![WeightWatchers]

shop *and* cook

70 delicious recipes complete with shopping lists

Tamsin Burnett-Hall

SIMON & SCHUSTER
A CBS COMPANY

First published in Great Britain by
Simon & Schuster UK Ltd, 2008
A CBS Company
Copyright © 2008, Weight Watchers International, Inc.
Simon & Schuster UK Ltd, Africa House,
64–78 Kingsway, London WC2B 6AH
This book is copyright under the
Berne Convention.
No reproduction without permission.
All rights reserved.
1 3 5 7 9 10 8 6 4 2

Weight Watchers, POINTS and Core Plan are trademarks of
Weight Watchers International, Inc., and are used under its control by
Weight Watchers (UK) Ltd.

Weight Watchers Publications Team
Jane Griffiths, Donna Watts, Nina McKerlie, Nina Bhogal and Eileen Thornton
Photography by Steve Baxter
Styling by Rachel Jukes
Food preparation and styling by Carol Tennant
Design and typesetting by Jane Humphrey
Printed and bound in China

A CIP catalogue for this book is available from the British Library

Pictured on the front cover: Pizza style bruschetta, page 84
Pictured on the back cover: clockwise from top to bottom, Garlic mushroom and goat's cheese pizza, page 58; Middle Eastern meatballs, page 44; Strawberry and banana crêpes, page 92
Pictured on the inside front flap: Baked summer fruits meringue, page 18
Pictured on the introduction: Chilli crab linguine, page 29

 POINTS® value logo: You'll find this easy to read **POINTS** value logo on every recipe throughout this book. The logo represents the number of **POINTS** values per serving each recipe contains. The easy to use **POINTS** Plan is designed to help you eat what you want, when you want – as long as you stay within your daily **POINTS** allowance – giving you the freedom to enjoy the food you love.

You'll find this distinctive **Core Plan™** logo on every recipe that can be followed freely on the **Core Plan**. These recipes contain only foods that form part of the **Core Plan**.

Ⓨ This symbol denotes a vegetarian recipe and assumes that, where relevant, free range eggs, vegetarian cheese, vegetarian virtually fat free fromage frais and vegetarian low fat crème fraîche are used. Virtually fat free fromage frais and low fat crème fraîche may contain traces of gelatine so they are not always vegetarian. Please check the labels.

❄ This symbol denotes a dish that can be frozen.

Recipe notes

Egg size Medium, unless otherwise stated.
All fruits and vegetables Medium sized unless otherwise stated.
Raw eggs Only the freshest eggs should be used. Pregnant women, the elderly and children should avoid recipes with eggs which are not fully cooked or raw.
Recipe timings These are approximate and meant to be guidelines. Please note that the preparation time includes all the steps up to and following the main cooking time(s).
Polyunsaturated margarine Use brands such as Flora Light, St Ivel Gold and Benecol Light.
Core Plan If following the **Core Plan** you have a limited allowance of 2 teaspoons of healthy oil a day (olive, sunflower, safflower, flaxseed, rapeseed) to use in recipes as you choose.

The days of half full pots of low fat crème fraîche, half a mango or left over egg whites sitting at the back of the fridge are over. *Shop and Cook* is a unique collection of recipes, where each chapter is designed to use a similar pool of ingredients so nothing is wasted. Shopping lists are made easy with the Kitchen Basics at the front of the book and the recipe-specific ingredients listed at the front of each chapter. All recipes serve four people but can easily be halved.

However, if you want to enjoy preparing different meals from the 6 chapters, there are 70 fantastic recipes to choose from. And there are over 30 recipes suitable for vegetarians as well.

There are delicious salads and soups to enjoy at lunchtime or as a light meal, pastas and meat dishes for a warming dinner and a range of scrumptious desserts to choose from. Each recipe has the ***POINTS*** values clearly marked and those suitable on the **Core Plan** have the distinctive **Core Plan** tick. You'll also find that the first 3 chapters are suitable on the **Core Plan**. So, whichever food plan you are following, there is something for you. All the recipes use fresh, healthy ingredients so you can relax and enjoy mealtimes, while staying on track with your weight loss.

We hope you enjoy *Shop and Cook* and find inspiration on every page.

Kitchen basics

Here's a list of ingredients which are always useful to have in the kitchen.

Baking and sweet ingredients

- Baking powder
- Bicarbonate of soda
- Cocoa powder
- Cornflour
- Custard, low fat
- Fruit, dried
- Honey
- Plain flour
- Porridge oats
- Reduced sugar jam including strawberry
- Self raising flour
- Sugar
- Sugar free jelly
- Vanilla extract

Basic cooking ingredients

- Artificial sweetener
- Black pepper
- Black peppercorns
- Gelatine
- Low fat cooking spray
- Olive oil
- Salt (preferably sea salt or low sodium)
- Stock cubes, vegetable, beef and chicken

Canned goods

- Baked beans, reduced sugar and salt
- Borlotti beans
- Butter beans
- Canned fruit, assorted, in natural juice
- Cannellini beans
- Chick peas
- Flageolet beans
- Kidney beans
- Lentils
- Tomatoes, chopped
- Tuna, canned in brine or in spring water

Condiments

- Balsamic vinegar
- Gravy granules
- Mayonnaise, extra light
- Mushrooms, dried e.g. porcini
- Mustard, wholegrain and English
- Olives
- Salad dressing, fat free
- Tomato ketchup
- Tomato purée

Dried herbs and spices

- Cayenne pepper
- Chilli powder
- Chinese 5 spice powder
- Cinnamon, ground
- Coriander, ground
- Cumin, ground
- Cumin seeds
- Curry powder
- Ginger, ground
- Mixed herbs, dried
- Mixed spice, ground
- Nutmeg
- Paprika

Dried pasta and noodles (preferably wholemeal)

- Egg noodles
- Pasta of your choice
- Rice noodles

Fresh ingredients

- Cheddar, reduced fat
- Eggs
- Fresh herbs
- Margarine, low fat polyunsaturated
- Soft cheese, low fat
- Yogurt, 0% fat Greek
- Yogurt, low fat fruit and plain

Fresh vegetables and fruit

- Carrots
- Fruit, fresh, in season
- Garlic
- Leeks
- Onions
- Potatoes
- Salad ingredients
- Tomatoes
- Vegetables, green, in season

Rice and grains

- Bulgur wheat
- Couscous, plain
- Rice, brown, long grain or basmati

Sauces

- Apple sauce
- Horseradish sauce
- Mint sauce
- Soy sauce
- Tabasco sauce
- Worcestershire sauce

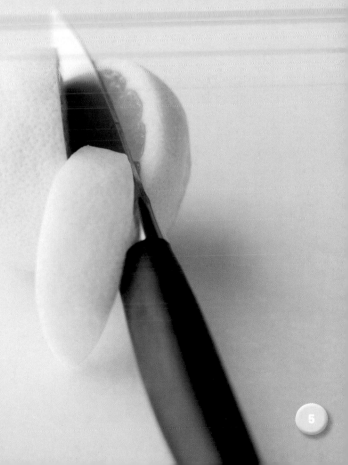

Planning your week ahead: Chapter one

Dairy

- Eggs, 9
- Fromage frais, low fat plain, 165 g
- Low fat soft cheese, 240 g
- Low fat soft cheese with garlic and herbs, 200 g
- Milk, skimmed, 600 ml
- Yogurt, Greek, 0% fat, 150 g

Dry and canned ingredients

- Black eyed beans, 1 x 410 g can
- Butter beans, 3 x 410 g cans
- Coffee, instant, 2 tbsp
- Egg noodles, dried, medium, 125 g
- Jelly, lemon and lime sugar free, 1 x 12 g sachet
- Lentils, red, dried, 150 g
- Pasta shells, dried, 450 g
- Pineapple slices in natural juice, 1 x 220 g can
- Pinto beans, 1 x 410 g can
- Rosemary, dried, 1 tsp
- Tomatoes, chopped, 1 x 400 g can

Fruit, vegetables and herbs

- Avocado, ripe, 1
- Basil, fresh, 1 x 25 g packet
- Beansprouts, 175 g
- Cherry tomatoes, 500 g
- Chives, fresh, 1 x 25 g packet
- Leeks, 300 g
- Mange tout, 150 g
- Mango, ripe, 1
- Mushrooms, large flat, 4
- Oranges, 2
- Peas, frozen, 150 g
- Peppers, green, red, yellow, 2 each
- Potatoes, 1 kg
- Root ginger, fresh, small knob (for 1 tsp)
- Spinach, young leaf, 200 g
- Summer fruits mix, frozen, 250 g
- Sweet potatoes, 800 g

Meat, fish and seafood

- Bacon, lean back and smoked, 8 rashers
- Beef medallion steaks, lean, 4 x 110 g
- Chicken thighs, skinless and boneless, 600 g
- Haddock, smoked, 500 g
- Lamb leg steaks, lean, 4 x 100 g
- Prawns, peeled and cooked, 250 g

And from your Kitchen Basics, you will need the following ingredients: artificial sweetener, black peppercorns, chicken stock cubes, chilli powder, cumin seeds, curry powder, fat free salad dressing, garlic, low fat cooking spray, onions, salt, soy sauce and wholegrain mustard.

Chinese prawn and noodle salad

Takes 10 minutes
12 POINTS values per recipe
209 calories per serving
Serves 4

A superb salad for a working lunch.

125 g (4½ oz) dried medium egg noodles
1 x 220 g can pineapple slices in natural juice, diced
2 tablespoons soy sauce
1 teaspoon grated root ginger
½ red pepper, de-seeded and sliced thinly
½ yellow pepper, de-seeded and sliced thinly
½ green pepper, de-seeded and sliced thinly
175 g (6 oz) beansprouts, rinsed
250 g (9 oz) cooked peeled prawns

❶ Bring a saucepan of water to the boil, add the noodles and cook for 5 minutes or according to the packet instructions until tender.
❷ Meanwhile, measure 4 tablespoons of juice from the pineapple can into a large bowl and stir in the soy sauce and grated ginger. Add the pineapple to the bowl along with the peppers and beansprouts.
❸ Drain the noodles and refresh in cold water. Snip into slightly shorter lengths using kitchen scissors, then mix the noodles and prawns into the pineapple and vegetables. Serve in bowls or take to work in a sealed container.

Butter bean and bacon soup

❄ **Takes 15 minutes**
14 POINTS values per recipe
286 calories per serving
Serves 4

A flavoursome soup that will keep you satisfied for several hours.

1 onion, chopped finely
2 garlic cloves, crushed
1 teaspoon dried rosemary
850 ml (1½ pints) chicken stock
low fat cooking spray
4 rashers smoked lean back bacon, cut into small strips
3 x 410 g cans butter beans, rinsed and drained
freshly ground black pepper

❶ Put the onion, garlic, rosemary and 150 ml (5 fl oz) of the stock in a large lidded saucepan. Cover, bring to the boil and simmer briskly for 5 minutes until softened.
❷ Meanwhile, spray a non stick frying pan with low fat cooking spray and fry the bacon for 2–3 minutes until browned and crisp. Set aside.
❸ Stir the beans and the rest of the stock into the pan with the onions. Cover, bring back to the boil and simmer for 3 minutes. Transfer to a blender or use a hand blender. Blend until smooth, adding freshly ground black pepper to taste. Ladle into warmed bowls and serve topped with the crispy bacon bits.

Ⓨ **Tip** For a vegetarian version, replace the bacon with four Quorn Deli Bacon Style Rashers, and use vegetable stock in place of chicken stock, for a **POINTS** value of 2½ per serving.

Egg and avocado pasta salad

Takes 20 minutes

19½ *POINTS* values per recipe

337 calories per serving

Serves 4

3 eggs

200 g (7 oz) dried pasta shells

150 g (5½ oz) mange tout, halved

1 ripe avocado

2 tablespoons snipped fresh chives

4 tablespoons fat free salad dressing

100 g (3½ oz) young leaf spinach

freshly ground black pepper

① Place the eggs in a small saucepan, cover with cold water and bring to the boil. Simmer for 6 minutes, then place in cold water to cool. Peel and cut into quarters.

② Meanwhile, bring another saucepan of water to the boil, cook the pasta for 12 minutes or according to the packet instructions. Add the mange tout and cook with the pasta during the final 2 minutes. Drain and rinse in cold water.

③ While the pasta is cooking, cut the avocado in half and remove the stone. Use a dessertspoon to scoop the avocado flesh from the skin in one piece, then cut into dice. Mix the avocado, chives and dressing together in a bowl, then stir in the drained pasta and mange tout, followed by the spinach. Add freshly ground pepper, to taste, and serve topped with the hard boiled eggs.

Cumin lamb with spinach dhal

Takes 30 minutes
20 POINTS values per recipe
323 calories per serving
Serves 4

Serve with 100 g (3½ oz) green beans per person, for no additional **POINTS** values.

150 g (5½ oz) dried red lentils, rinsed
1 onion, chopped finely
2 teaspoons curry powder
3 teaspoons cumin seeds
600 ml (1 pint) boiling water
1 x 410 g can pinto beans, rinsed and drained
4 x 100 g (3½ oz) lean lamb leg steaks
low fat cooking spray
100 g (3½ oz) young leaf spinach
freshly ground black pepper

❶ To make the dhal, place the lentils, onion, curry powder and 1 teaspoon of cumin seeds in a lidded non stick saucepan with the boiling water. Cover and bring back to the boil then simmer for 15 minutes. Stir in the pinto beans, re-cover the pan and cook for a further 5 minutes.

❷ Meanwhile, lightly season the lamb steaks with freshly ground black pepper and press the remaining 2 teaspoons of cumin seeds on to the meat. Heat a non stick frying pan, spray with low fat cooking spray and cook the lamb for 3–4 minutes on each side over a high heat until cooked to your liking.

❸ Stir the spinach into the pan of lentils until wilted. Ladle the dhal into deep plates and serve with the lamb.

Spicy chicken and black eyed bean stew

❄ **Takes 15 minutes to prepare, 20 minutes to cook**
30½ *POINTS* values per recipe
460 calories per serving
Serves 4

A hearty, spicy stew that is delicious with broccoli, for no additional *POINTS* values.

low fat cooking spray
600 g (1 lb 5 oz) skinless boneless chicken thigh fillets, diced
1 large onion, chopped roughly
1½ green peppers, de-seeded and chopped roughly
¼ teaspoon hot chilli powder
1 x 400 g can chopped tomatoes
1 x 410 g can black eyed beans, rinsed and drained
salt and freshly ground black pepper
150 g (5½ oz) 0% fat Greek yogurt, to serve

❶ Heat a flameproof lidded casserole and spray with low fat cooking spray. Brown the chicken for 5–6 minutes over a high heat, then remove to a plate.
❷ Spray the casserole again with low fat cooking spray and cook the onion and pepper for 4 minutes. Stir in the chilli powder and the chicken, then add the chopped tomatoes and beans. Season, cover and simmer for 20 minutes.
❸ Serve the soup topped with the yogurt, in warm bowls.

❤ **Tip** You can replace the chicken with 600 g (1 lb 5 oz) Quorn Chicken Style Pieces to make a vegetarian version of this recipe, for 3½ *POINTS* values per serving.

Smoky fish pie

❄ **Takes 20 minutes to prepare, 20 minutes to cook**
33 *POINTS* values per recipe
465 calories per serving
Serves 4

1 kg (2 lb 4 oz) potatoes, peeled and chopped roughly
low fat cooking spray
4 rashers smoked lean back bacon, chopped
300 ml (10 fl oz) skimmed milk
500 g (1 lb 2 oz) smoked haddock, skinned and diced
150 g (5½ oz) frozen peas
200 g (7 oz) low fat soft cheese
125 g (4½ oz) low fat plain fromage frais
1 teaspoon wholegrain mustard

❶ Preheat the oven to Gas Mark 6/200°C/fan oven 180°C. Cook the potatoes in boiling water for 12–15 minutes until tender.
❷ Meanwhile, spray a non stick frying pan with low fat cooking spray. Fry the bacon for 2 minutes until browned. Transfer to a baking dish. In a saucepan, bring the milk to a simmer, add the haddock and poach for 4 minutes. Using a slotted spoon, transfer the haddock to the baking dish with the bacon and then add the peas to the milk and bring back to a simmer. Strain the milk into a measuring jug and set aside. Tip the peas into the baking dish and mix everything together gently.
❸ Mix the soft cheese with the fromage frais and mustard. Gradually mix in 100 ml (3½ fl oz) of the poaching milk to make a sauce, then pour over the fish mixture.
❹ Drain the potatoes and mash with 100 ml (3½ fl oz) of the poaching milk, discarding the rest. Cover the top of the fish with the potato mixture. Spritz with low fat cooking spray and bake for 20 minutes in the oven until the top is browned and the sauce is bubbling.

A homely, warming fish pie that's perfect served with lightly cooked cabbage and steamed carrots, for no extra *POINTS* values.

8½ POINTS VALUE

Steak, mushrooms and sweet potato chips

Takes 30 minutes
21½ *POINTS* values per recipe
426 calories per serving
Serves 4

Lightly cooked but still crunchy sugar snap peas go well with this recipe, for no additional *POINTS* values.

800 g (1 lb 11 oz) sweet potatoes, peeled
low fat cooking spray
4 large flat mushrooms
300 g (10½ oz) leeks, trimmed and sliced
125 g (4½ oz) low fat soft cheese with garlic and herbs
4 x 110 g (4 oz) lean beef medallion steaks
salt and freshly ground black pepper

❶ Preheat the oven to Gas Mark 7/220°C/fan oven 200°C.

❷ Cut the sweet potatoes into chunky chips, lightly spray with low fat cooking spray and spread out on a baking tray. Place on a high oven shelf and cook for 25 minutes, turning halfway through.

❸ Once the sweet potatoes are in the oven, remove the stalks from the mushrooms and set the stalks aside. Season the mushrooms and place them, open cup side up, in a roasting tin. Spray with low fat cooking spray, cover with foil and bake below the potatoes for 7 minutes until tender.

❹ Meanwhile, to make the filling, chop the mushroom stalks. Spray a lidded, non stick saucepan with low fat cooking spray. Add the leeks and stalks with 3 tablespoons of water and cook, covered, for 3 minutes until softened. Stir in the low fat soft cheese. Take the

mushrooms out of the oven, remove the foil and spoon in the filling. Return the uncovered mushrooms to the oven for 10 minutes until lightly browned.

❺ Meanwhile, spray a non stick frying pan with low fat cooking spray. Cook the steaks for 3–4 minutes on each side, or until cooked to your liking. Serve with the stuffed mushrooms and sweet potato chips.

🅨 **Tip** To make this dish vegetarian, simply double the amount of leeks and soft cheese as well as the amount of mushrooms to replace the beef. Serve two stuffed mushrooms per person with the sweet potato chips. This will be 4 *POINTS* values per serving.

Caramelised tomato and pepper pasta

Takes 30 minutes
14 *POINTS* values per recipe
307 calories per serving
Serves 4

Serve with a large, mixed, zero *POINTS* value salad.

1½ red peppers, de-seeded and diced
1½ yellow peppers, de-seeded and diced
low fat cooking spray
500 g (1 lb 2 oz) cherry tomatoes, halved
3 garlic cloves, crushed
4 tablespoons freshly shredded basil
250 g (9 oz) dried pasta shells
75 g (2¾ oz) low fat soft cheese with garlic and herbs
freshly ground black pepper

❶ Preheat the oven to Gas Mark 7/220°C/fan oven 200°C.

❷ Spread the peppers out on a large baking tray. Lightly coat with low fat cooking spray, then place in the oven on the top shelf for 15 minutes.

❸ Place the tomatoes in a roasting tin, scatter with the garlic, 2 tablespoons of the basil and season with freshly ground black pepper. Mist with low fat cooking spray and place in the oven below the peppers. Cook for 10 minutes. Stir both trays halfway through.

❹ Bring a saucepan of water to the boil, add the pasta and cook for 10–12 minutes or according to the packet instructions until tender then drain. Mix the pasta with the low fat soft cheese, the peppers and remaining basil. Gently stir in the tomatoes and their juices and serve in warmed bowls.

Mango and citrus jellies

Takes 10 minutes + 2–3 hours chilling
3 *POINTS* values per recipe
42 calories per serving
Serves 4

A perfectly refreshing dessert.

300 ml (10 fl oz) boiling water
1 x 12 g sachet lemon and lime sugar free jelly
1 ripe mango
4 teaspoons low fat plain fromage frais, to serve

❶ Put the boiling water in a measuring jug, sprinkle over the jelly crystals and stir to dissolve.
❷ Peel the mango, then slice off one cheek and cut the flesh into small dice. Divide between four ramekins or glasses. Cut the remaining mango flesh away from the central stone, chop roughly and using a blender or hand blender, blend to a purée. Mix into the jelly, then make up to 600 ml (1 pint) with cold water. Pour over the diced mango, cover and chill for 2–3 hours until set.
❸ Serve each jelly topped with 1 teaspoon of fromage frais.

Coffee custards

Takes 10 minutes to prepare, 15 minutes to cook
7½ *POINTS* values per recipe
138 calories per serving
Serves 4

These luxurious baked custards can be enjoyed warm or chilled depending on your mood – and the weather.

300 ml (10 fl oz) skimmed milk
2 eggs plus 2 yolks, beaten
40 g (1½ oz) low fat soft cheese
2 tablespoons instant coffee
2 tablespoons artificial sweetener
a kettle full of boiling water

❶ Preheat the oven to Gas Mark 3/160°C/fan oven 140°C. In a non stick saucepan, bring the milk to simmering point.
❷ Meanwhile in a mixing bowl, gradually beat the eggs and yolks into the soft cheese, using a wooden spoon. Dissolve the instant coffee and sweetener in 1 tablespoon of boiling water then add this to the egg mixture.
❸ Slowly mix in the hot milk, stirring until smooth. Pour the coffee custard through a strainer (to remove any eggy threads) into four ramekins set in a roasting tin. Pour the remaining boiling water into the tin so that it comes halfway up the ramekins. Bake in the oven for 15 minutes until the custards feel fairly firm, but are still slightly wobbly in the centre.
❹ Lift the ramekins out of the hot water using a fish slice. Serve warm, or cool and chill in the fridge if desired.

Tip You can use the left over egg whites to make the Baked summer fruits meringue (opposite).

Baked summer fruits meringue

Takes 10 minutes to prepare, 10 minutes to cook
2½ *POINTS* values per recipe
62 calories per serving
Serves 4

This is deliciously summery but can still be made in the depths of winter as it uses frozen fruit.

2 oranges
250 g (9 oz) frozen summer fruits mix
3 tablespoons artificial sweetener
2 egg whites

❶ Preheat the oven to Gas Mark 4/180°C/fan oven 160°C.
❷ Grate the zest from half of one orange and reserve. Place the frozen summer fruits in a lidded non stick saucepan with 1 tablespoon of sweetener. Cover and simmer for 3 minutes until juicy then remove from the heat.
❸ Meanwhile, peel both oranges and cut into thick slices. Then cut the orange slices into quarters and mix into the summer fruits. Divide the fruit between four ramekins.
❹ Whisk the egg whites to soft peaks in a clean mixing bowl then add the remaining 2 tablespoons of sweetener and whisk again until the meringue is stiff and shiny. Spoon on top of the fruits, swirl decoratively and scatter with the reserved orange zest.
❺ Bake for 8–10 minutes until the meringues are lightly browned and puffed up. Serve immediately.

Tip You can use the left over egg yolks to make the Coffee custards (opposite).

This meringue topped fruity dessert looks
impressive and tastes heavenly.

inspiring

Planning your week ahead: Chapter two

Dairy

- Eggs, 6
- Fromage frais, very low fat plain, 4 tbsp
- Low fat soft cheese, 200 g
- Milk, skimmed, 425 ml
- Yogurt, Greek, 0% fat, 150 g
- Yogurt, low fat, natural, 100 g
- Yogurt, low fat, peach flavour, 150 g

Dry and canned ingredients

- Cannellini beans, 2 x 410 g cans
- Cinnamon stick, 1
- Linguine, dried, 250 g
- Passata, 1 x 700 g jar
- Peach slices in natural juice, 1 x 411 g can
- Polenta, dried, 75 g

- Porcini mushrooms, ½ x 15 g packet
- Rice, brown, 175 g
- Sage, dried, ½ tsp
- Spaghetti, dried quick cook, 200 g
- Tagliatelle, dried, 250 g
- Tomatoes, chopped, 3 x 400 g cans
- Vanilla pod, ½
- Wholewheat crispbreads, 3

Fruit, vegetables and herbs

- Avocado, 1
- Basil, fresh, 1 x 25 g packet
- Blueberries, frozen, 125 g
- Chilli, green, 1
- Chilli, red, 1
- Clementines, 8
- Coriander, fresh, 1 x 25 g packet

- Courgettes, 450 g
- Leek, 1
- Lemons, 2
- Lime, 1
- Mushrooms, closed cup, 150 g
- Peppers, 2 red and 1 green
- Potatoes, 1.2 kg
- Potatoes, new, 600 g
- Potatoes, red skinned, 800 g
- Radishes, 1 packet
- Raspberries, frozen, 125 g
- Red onion, 1
- Root ginger, fresh, a small knob (for 2 tsp)
- Salad leaves, crisp mixed, 140 g
- Spring onions, 2 bunches
- Sweetcorn, frozen, 125 g
- Thyme, fresh, 1 x 25 g packet

Meat, fish, seafood and vegetarian alternatives

- Bacon, back lean, 4 rashers
- Beef escalopes, lean, 450 g
- Chicken breasts, skinless and boneless, 2 x 150 g
- Crab meat, 2 x 170 g cans
- Mackerel fillets, smoked, 300 g
- Parma ham, 4 slices
- Pork mince, lean, 750 g
- Quorn mince, 350 g
- Turkey breast steaks, 4 x 125 g

And from your Kitchen Basics, you will need the following ingredients: artificial sweetener, black peppercorns, chilli powder, dried mixed herbs, garlic, gelatine, gravy granules, ground cinnamon, ground cumin, horseradish sauce, low fat cooking spray, onions, salt, vegetable stock cubes and wholegrain mustard.

Mexican chicken and rice salad

Takes 35 minutes
21 *POINTS* values per recipe
358 calories per serving
Serves 4

A good lunchbox salad.

175 g (6 oz) brown rice
125 g (4½ oz) frozen sweetcorn
2 x 150 g (5½ oz) skinless boneless chicken breasts,
    sliced into finger width strips
juice of a lime
1 tablespoon ground cumin
½ teaspoon chilli powder
1 red pepper, de-seeded and diced
1 avocado, peeled, stoned and diced
salt and freshly ground black pepper

❶ Bring a saucepan of water to the boil, add the rice and cook for 25 minutes or until tender, adding the frozen sweetcorn for the last 5 minutes of the cooking time.
❷ Meanwhile, toss the chicken with half the lime juice, cumin and chilli powder. Set aside for 5 minutes while you preheat the grill to medium high.
❸ Grill the chicken strips for 10 minutes, turning after 5 minutes, until cooked through. Leave to cool.
❹ Drain the rice and sweetcorn and rinse in cold water, then drain well again. Mix together with the rest of the lime juice, the diced pepper and avocado. Season to taste. Slice the chicken fillets across to make little chunks and serve on top of the rice salad.

Ⓥ **Tip** You can easily make a vegetarian version by replacing the chicken with 300 g (10½ oz) Quorn Chicken Style Pieces. The *POINTS* values will remain the same.

Spanish omelette

Ⓥ Takes 25 minutes
12 *POINTS* values per recipe
239 calories per serving
Serves 4

This hearty omelette can be served warm straight from the pan, or it can be cooled for a packed lunch or picnic. Either way, it is great served with a crisp, zero *POINTS* value green salad.

low fat cooking spray
1 onion, sliced
1 red pepper, de-seeded and sliced
1 green pepper, de-seeded and sliced
125 ml (4 fl oz) vegetable stock
400 g (14 oz) potatoes, peeled and diced
6 eggs, beaten
salt and freshly ground black pepper

❶ Heat a lidded non stick frying pan, spray with low fat cooking spray then stir fry the onion and peppers for 5 minutes until coloured. Add the stock, cover partially and simmer rapidly for 5 minutes until the vegetables are tender and the liquid has evaporated.
❷ Meanwhile, bring a saucepan of water to the boil and cook the potatoes for 8–10 minutes until tender, then drain. Stir the potatoes into the frying pan with the peppers and onion.
❸ Season the eggs then pour into the frying pan. Shake to settle the contents and cook over a gentle heat for 5 minutes until most of the egg has set. Preheat the grill to a medium setting.
❹ Transfer to the grill, protecting the handle of the pan from the heat, and cook for 3 minutes to set the top. Cut into wedges and serve warm or cold.

Sweet tomato and basil soup

Ⓨ ✷ **Takes 15 minutes**

1 *POINTS* value per recipe

84 calories per serving

Serves 4

low fat cooking spray

1 leek, trimmed and sliced

600 ml (1 pint) vegetable stock

1 x 700 g jar passata

4 tablespoons chopped fresh basil, plus extra leaves to garnish

2 teaspoons artificial sweetener

freshly ground black pepper

4 tablespoons very low fat plain fromage frais, to serve

❶ Spray a non stick lidded saucepan with low fat cooking spray. Add the leek, cover and cook for 2 minutes. Add 3 tablespoons of stock, cover again and cook for 3 more minutes until softened.

❷ Pour in the rest of the stock and the passata. Season with freshly ground black pepper, cover and bring to a simmer. Cook for 5 minutes and then transfer to a blender, or use a hand blender, and blend with the basil and sweetener.

❸ Serve topped with fromage frais and basil leaves.

Smoked mackerel and potato salad

Takes 15 minutes
28 *POINTS* values per recipe
371 calories per serving
Serves 4

600 g (1 lb 5 oz) new potatoes, cut into chunky dice
100 g (3½ oz) low fat natural yogurt
1½ tablespoons horseradish sauce
1 tablespoon wholegrain mustard
300 g (10½ oz) smoked mackerel fillets
140 g (5 oz) crisp mixed salad leaves
6 radishes, trimmed and sliced
freshly ground black pepper

❶ Bring a saucepan of water to the boil and cook the potatoes for 10–12 minutes until tender.
❷ Meanwhile, to make the dressing, mix the yogurt together with the horseradish sauce, mustard and freshly ground black pepper, then set aside. Remove the skin from the mackerel fillets and break the fish into large flakes.
❸ Divide the salad leaves between four plates and scatter the radishes and smoked mackerel on top.
❹ Drain the potatoes and mix with the yogurt dressing, then spoon on top of each salad to serve

Garlicky courgette spaghetti

Y Takes 15 minutes
15 *POINTS* values per recipe
245 calories per serving
Serves 4

This sauce has a lovely fresh flavour and the low fat soft cheese makes it rich and creamy. A tomato salad makes a good accompaniment, for no additional *POINTS* values.

200 g (7 oz) dried quick cook spaghetti
low fat cooking spray
450 g (1 lb) courgettes, grated coarsely
1 red chilli, de-seeded and diced
2 garlic cloves, crushed
200 g (7 oz) low fat soft cheese
grated zest and juice of ½ a lemon
salt and freshly ground black pepper

❶ Bring a saucepan of water to the boil and cook the pasta for 5 minutes or according to the packet instructions until tender.
❷ Meanwhile, heat a large non stick frying pan, spray with low fat cooking spray and then stir fry the courgettes, chilli and garlic for 4 minutes until softened. Stir in the soft cheese, lemon zest and lemon juice. Season to taste.
❸ Drain the pasta in a colander, then toss with the courgette sauce in the frying pan. Serve immediately in warmed bowls.

Turkey roulades with mini roasties

Takes 15 minutes to prepare, 25 minutes to cook
30 *POINTS* values per recipe
403 calories per serving
Serves 4

800 g (1 lb 11 oz) red skinned potatoes, unpeeled and diced
1 red onion, half chopped finely and half chopped roughly
250 g (9 oz) lean minced pork
1 wholewheat crispbread, crumbled
½ teaspoon dried sage
low fat cooking spray
4 x 125 g (4½ oz) turkey breast steaks, flattened with a rolling pin if thick
4 slices Parma ham
4 teaspoons gravy granules
250 ml (9 fl oz) boiling water
freshly ground black pepper

❶ Preheat the oven to Gas Mark 6/200°C/fan oven 180°C.
❷ Cook the potatoes in boiling water for 5 minutes. To make the stuffing for the roulades, mix the finely chopped half of the onion with the pork, crispbread, sage and freshly ground black pepper.
❸ Drain the potatoes and shake to roughen up the edges, then spread out on a baking tray. Spray lightly with low fat cooking spray then roast in the oven for a total of 25 minutes, adding the roughly chopped half of the onion to the potatoes after 15 minutes.
❹ Meanwhile, spread the stuffing over the turkey. Roll up. Tuck the Parma ham around each roulade. Place in a roasting tin, spritz with low fat cooking spray and roast for 20 minutes below the potatoes.
❺ Make up the gravy granules with the boiling water and serve with turkey roulades and mini roasties.

A mid week version of Sunday roast, without the work. Serve with Chantenay carrots and broccoli to complete the meal, for no additional *POINTS* values.

Quorn and mushroom ragu

Y ❄ (sauce only)
Takes 20 minutes
17 *POINTS* values per recipe
342 calories per serving
Serves 4

½ x 15 g packet dried porcini mushrooms
200 ml (7 fl oz) boiling water
low fat cooking spray
1 onion, chopped
2 garlic cloves, crushed
150 g (5½ oz) closed cup mushrooms, quartered
1 x 400 g can chopped tomatoes
1 teaspoon dried mixed herbs
350 g (12 oz) Quorn mince
250 g (9 oz) dried tagliatelle
freshly ground black pepper

❶ Soak the porcini mushrooms in the boiling water in a small bowl according to the packet instructions.

❷ Spray a large lidded non stick saucepan with low fat cooking spray. Add the onion, cover and cook for 4 minutes, adding a splash of water, if needed, to prevent it from burning. Stir in the garlic and closed cup mushrooms, cover the pan again and cook for 2–3 minutes more.

❸ Add the tomatoes, herbs and freshly ground black pepper to taste. Tip in the porcini mushrooms and their soaking liquid, except for the very last bit which may be rather sandy. Stir the Quorn mince into the sauce, cover and simmer for 12 minutes.

❹ Meanwhile, bring a saucepan of water to the boil and cook the pasta for 8–10 minutes or according to the packet instructions. Drain and serve topped with the Quorn and mushroom ragu.

Chilli crab linguine

Takes 15 minutes

15 *POINTS* values per recipe

288 calories per serving

Serves 4

This lightly spiced dish is a fusion of flavours and cuisines. The aromatic ginger and coriander complement the sweetness of the crab beautifully.

250 g (9 oz) dried linguine

low fat cooking spray

1 x 25 g packet fresh coriander, stalks chopped finely and
    leaves torn up roughly

1 green chilli, de-seeded and diced

2 teaspoons grated fresh root ginger

1 x 400 g can chopped tomatoes

2 x 170 g cans crab meat in brine, drained

freshly ground black pepper

❶ Bring a saucepan of water to the boil and cook the pasta for 10–12 minutes or according to the packet instructions until tender. Drain.

❷ Meanwhile, heat a medium non stick saucepan, spray with low fat cooking spray and gently fry the coriander stalks, chilli and ginger for 1 minute to release the flavours. Tip in the tomatoes and add freshly ground black pepper. Simmer for 8 minutes. Stir in half the crab then toss with the pasta.

❸ Divide between four warmed bowls and top with the rest of the crab. Scatter generously with the coriander leaves and serve.

Lemony pork meatballs and spring onion mash

Takes 25 minutes

28½ *POINTS* values per recipe

337 calories per serving

Serves 4

These delicious meatballs in gravy go particularly well with green beans, for no additional ***POINTS*** values.

800 g (1 lb 11 oz) potatoes, peeled and chopped roughly

2 wholewheat crispbreads, crumbled

125 ml (4 fl oz) skimmed milk

zest of a lemon and juice from half

500 g (1 lb 2 oz) lean minced pork

low fat cooking spray

4 teaspoons gravy granules

250 ml (9 fl oz) boiling water

1 bunch spring onions, chopped

salt and freshly ground black pepper

❶ Bring a saucepan of water to the boil and cook the potatoes for 12–15 minutes until tender.

❷ Meanwhile, place the crispbread crumbs in a mixing bowl and moisten with 1 tablespoon of the milk. Put the lemon zest in the bowl and mix it together with the pork mince and seasoning. Shape into twenty small meatballs.

❸ Spray a non stick frying pan with low fat cooking spray and cook the meatballs for 12 minutes over a medium heat, turning frequently, until browned and cooked through.

❹ Make up the gravy granules with the boiling water then pour this over the meatballs. Add the lemon juice to taste. Simmer for 3 minutes, shaking the pan occasionally to coat the meatballs in the sauce.

❺ Drain the potatoes in a colander. Spray the same saucepan used to cook the potatoes with low fat cooking spray and cook the spring onions for 2 minutes. Add the rest of the milk and heat through, then return the potatoes to the pan and mash until smooth. Serve with the meatballs and sauce.

Seared beef with amatriciana sauce

Takes 25 minutes
20½ *POINTS* values per recipe
373 calories per serving
Serves 4

low fat cooking spray
4 rashers lean back bacon, chopped roughly
1 bunch spring onions, sliced
4 garlic cloves, crushed
1 x 400 g can chopped tomatoes
1 tablespoon fresh thyme leaves
100 ml (3½ fl oz) vegetable stock
2 x 410 g cans cannellini beans, rinsed and drained
450 g (1 lb) lean beef escalopes
salt and freshly ground black pepper

❶ To make the sauce, spray a non stick saucepan with low fat cooking spray and heat until hot. Fry the bacon for 3 minutes. Add the spring onions and two garlic cloves. Cook for 2 minutes more before stirring in the tomatoes and season with freshly ground black pepper. Bring to a simmer and cook for 8–10 minutes, uncovered, to thicken the sauce.

❷ Meanwhile, spray a separate, lidded non stick saucepan with low fat cooking spray and fry the remaining garlic and the thyme for 1–2 minutes. Mix in the stock and the beans. Cover and simmer for 5 minutes, then mash together with a potato masher. Season to taste.

❸ Spray a non stick frying pan with low fat cooking spray and pan fry the beef escalopes for 2 minutes on each side. Make a bed of bean mash on each plate, sit the beef escalopes on top and serve with the sauce spooned over.

Peach creams

Takes 10 minutes + 2 hours chilling
5½ *POINTS* values per recipe
102 calories per serving
Serves 4

300 ml (10 fl oz) skimmed milk
1 x 12 g sachet gelatine
2 tablespoons artificial sweetener
1 x 411 g can peach slices in natural juice, drained and 2 slices reserved
150 g (5½ oz) low fat peach yogurt

❶ In a small bowl, pour in 4 tablespoons of the milk and sprinkle the gelatine over the milk. Leave to soak. Gently heat the remaining milk in a saucepan. Once it reaches simmering point, remove from the heat and stir in the soaked gelatine and sweetener until dissolved. Leave to cool for 5–10 minutes.

❷ Blend the peaches in a blender or use a hand blender, to make a purée. In a bowl, mix with the peach yogurt, then gradually mix in the cooled milk mixture until smooth. Pour into four dessert glasses, cover and chill for about 2 hours or until set.

❸ Cut the two reserved peach slices in half and use to decorate the tops of the peach creams before serving.

Spiced poached clementines

Y Takes 15 minutes + 30 minutes cooling
2 *POINTS* values per recipe
51 calories per serving
Serves 4

350 ml (12 fl oz) boiling water
juice of ½ a lemon
½ vanilla pod, split
1 cinnamon stick
2 tablespoons artificial sweetener
8 clementines, peeled, removing any thick white
   pithy bits

❶ In a large non stick saucepan, which will hold the clementines snugly, bring the boiling water, lemon juice, vanilla pod, cinnamon stick and artificial sweetener to a simmer.

❷ Add the clementines immediately to the simmering syrup and reduce the heat to a very gentle simmer. Cook for 5 minutes, turning the clementines over halfway through.

❸ Lift the clementines out using a draining spoon and transfer to a shallow dish. Boil the syrup quickly for 5 minutes to reduce it and concentrate the flavour, then pour through a strainer over the fruit. Discard the whole spices.

❹ Cool to room temperature for 30 minutes and serve. Alternatively, once cool, cover with clingfilm and chill the clementines in the fridge until ready to serve.

Sweet polenta wedges with warm berries

Y Takes 10 minutes + 15–20 minutes cooling
6½ *POINTS* values per recipe
118 calories per serving
Serves 4

a pinch of salt
75 g (2¾ oz) dried polenta
3 tablespoons artificial sweetener
low fat cooking spray
125 g (4½ oz) frozen raspberries
125 g (4½ oz) frozen blueberries
½ teaspoon ground cinnamon, plus extra to dust
150 g (5½ oz) 0% fat Greek yogurt, to serve

❶ In a non stick saucepan, bring 300 ml (10 fl oz) water to the boil, adding a pinch of salt. Tip in the polenta and quickly stir until smooth. Cook gently for 2 minutes, stirring occasionally until thickened and similar in consistency to porridge. Stir in 1½ tablespoons of sweetener, then turn the polenta out on to a side plate that has been lightly coated with low fat cooking spray. Smooth the top with the back of a spoon. Leave to cool and set for 15–20 minutes.

❷ When cool, cut the polenta into eight wedges, as if a cake. Spray a non stick frying pan with low fat cooking spray and then fry for 2½ minutes on each side over a high heat, until crisp and golden.

❸ Meanwhile, in a lidded saucepan, cook the frozen berries with the cinnamon and remaining sweetener, for 5 minutes until juicy and hot.

❹ Spoon the warm berries over the crisp polenta wedges and serve topped with the yogurt, sprinkled with a dusting of cinnamon.

Polenta is generally used for savoury dishes, but cooked this way, it also makes a delectable dessert.

tasty

Planning your week ahead: Chapter three

Dairy

- Cottage cheese, low fat, natural, 250 g
- Eggs, 2
- Fromage frais, low fat plain, 100 g
- Milk, skimmed, 300 ml
- Yogurt, Greek, 0% fat, 150 g
- Yogurt, low fat, smooth toffee flavour, 400 g
- Yogurt, low fat, vanilla flavour, 200 g

Dry and canned ingredients

- Black eyed beans, 2 x 410 g cans
- Chick peas, 1 x 410 g can
- Conchigliette, dried, 150 g
- Couscous, plain, 110 g
- Jelly, sugar free raspberry, 1 x 12 g sachet
- Rice noodles, dried, 250 g
- Tomatoes, chopped, 2 x 400 g cans
- Wholewheat crispbreads, 10

Fruit, vegetables and herbs

- Aubergine, 1
- Bananas, small, 4
- Beansprouts, 250 g
- Broccoli, 150 g
- Chilli, red, 1
- Coriander, fresh, 1 x 25 g packet
- Courgettes, 3
- Cucumber, 75 g
- Green beans, 350 g
- Leek, 1
- Lemons, 3
- Limes, 2
- Mango, large, 1
- Mixed summer berries (raspberries, strawberries, blackcurrants), 350 g
- Papaya, 1
- Parsley, fresh, 1 x 25 g packet
- Peppers, 2 red, 1 yellow, 1 green
- Pineapple, fresh, 1
- Potatoes, 300 g
- Raspberries, fresh, 250 g
- Red onion, 1
- Root ginger, fresh, a small knob (for 1 tbsp)
- Salad leaves, Italian style, 60 g
- Sweetcorn, frozen, 150 g
- Tomatoes, ripe, 5 (of which 2 are optional on p.38)

Meat, fish and seafood

- Beef medallion steak, lean, 400 g
- Chicken breasts, skinless and boneless, 4 x 150 g
- Ham, smoked, 110 g
- Lamb mince, lean, 500 g
- Prawns, peeled and cooked, 300 g
- Salmon fillets, skinless, 4 x 125 g

And from your Kitchen Basics, you will need the following ingredients: balsamic vinegar, black peppercorns, cayenne pepper, curry powder, dried mixed herbs, garlic, ground cinnamon, ground cumin, ground ginger, low fat cooking spray, onions, salt, soy sauce and vegetable stock cubes.

Zingy courgette and potato soup

Y ❄ Takes 10 minutes to prepare, 10–15 minutes to cook

4½ *POINTS* values per recipe

104 calories per serving

Serves 4

A fresh-tasting, summery soup.

700 ml (1¼ pints) vegetable stock
1 leek, sliced
2 courgettes, diced
300 g (10½ oz) potatoes, peeled and diced
grated zest and juice of a lemon
300 ml (10 fl oz) skimmed milk
freshly ground black pepper

❶ In a large lidded saucepan, pour in 4 tablespoons of the stock, add the sliced leek and cook, covered, for 2 minutes until starting to soften.
❷ Add the rest of the stock, the courgettes, potatoes and lemon zest. Bring to the boil, cover and simmer for 10–15 minutes until the vegetables are tender.
❸ Add the milk, then in a blender or with a hand blender, blend the soup until smooth. Stir in the lemon juice and some freshly ground black pepper to taste just before serving.

Ham and sweetcorn pasta lunchbox

Takes 15 minutes

13½ *POINTS* values per recipe

239 calories per serving

Serves 4

Here's an ideal pasta salad for lunch which can be thrown together while you are cooking supper the night before.

150 g (5½ oz) dried conchigliette (mini pasta shells)
150 g (5½ oz) small florets of broccoli
150 g (5½ oz) frozen sweetcorn
150 g (5½ oz) low fat natural cottage cheese
110 g (4 oz) smoked ham, diced
60 g (2 oz) Italian style salad leaves
salt and freshly ground black pepper
2 ripe tomatoes, sliced, to serve (optional)

❶ Bring a saucepan of water to the boil and cook the pasta for 5 minutes.
❷ Add the broccoli florets and sweetcorn to the pasta and cook for a further 5 minutes. Drain and rinse in cold water.
❸ Return to the pan. Toss the pasta and vegetables together with the cottage cheese and smoked ham, adding seasoning to taste. Divide between four lunch boxes. Top with the salad leaves but wait to mix them in until just before eating. Alternatively, toss in the salad leaves and serve on plates with tomato slices.

Prawn pâté
with crispbreads

Takes 5 minutes
13½ *POINTS* values per recipe
130 calories per serving
Serves 4

Ideal for a super quick meal. And it's so good you'll still feel like you're spoiling yourself.

300 g (10½ oz) peeled and cooked prawns
100 g (3½ oz) low fat natural cottage cheese
grated zest and juice of ½ a small lemon
a pinch of cayenne pepper
8 wholewheat crispbreads
75 g (2¾ oz) cucumber, sliced thinly
salt and freshly ground black pepper

❶ Reserve 50 g (1¾ oz) of the prawns to garnish, then place the rest of the prawns in a food processor with the cottage cheese, lemon zest and juice and cayenne pepper. Whiz to a thick paste. Season to taste.
❷ Spread the pâté on to the crispbread and top with the sliced cucumber and reserved prawns.

Vietnamese beef and noodle stir fry

Takes 15 minutes
20½ *POINTS* values per recipe
432 calories per serving
Serves 4

If you like it extra hot, leave the seeds in the chilli.

250 g (9 oz) dried rice noodles
low fat cooking spray
400 g (14 oz) lean beef medallion steak, sliced thinly
1 red onion, sliced thinly
2 garlic cloves, sliced
1 red chilli, de-seeded and sliced
250 g (9 oz) beansprouts, rinsed and drained
juice of ½ a lime
3 tablespoons soy sauce
½ x 25 g packet fresh coriander, sprigs left whole

❶ Bring a saucepan of water to the boil and add the noodles. Return to the boil then remove immediately from the heat. Leave to stand for 3 minutes while the noodles soften, then drain and rinse in cold water.

❷ Meanwhile, heat a wok or large non stick frying pan and spray with low fat cooking spray. Stir fry the sliced steak over a high heat for 3 minutes, then transfer to a plate.

❸ Add the onion, garlic and chilli to the pan and stir fry for 2 minutes. Mix in the beansprouts, followed by the noodles, beef, lime juice and soy sauce. Stir fry for 2 minutes until piping hot and well mixed. Mix in the sprigs of coriander just before serving.

41

Spicy bean cakes

Ⓨ ❄ Takes 30 minutes
9½ *POINTS* values per recipe
231 calories per serving
Serves 4

low fat cooking spray
2 onions, 1½ sliced finely and ½ chopped finely
1 tablespoon freshly grated root ginger
2 tablespoons balsamic vinegar
200 ml (7 fl oz) boiling water
1 red pepper, de-seeded and diced
2 x 410 g cans black eyed beans, rinsed and drained
1 egg, beaten
2 teaspoons curry powder
salt and freshly ground black pepper

❶ To make the onion relish, spray a non stick lidded saucepan with low fat cooking spray. Fry the sliced onions for 5 minutes. Add half the ginger, the balsamic vinegar and the boiling water. Cover and simmer for 5 minutes, then remove the lid. Cook rapidly for a further 10 minutes until the onions are tender and almost all of the liquid has evaporated.

❷ Meanwhile, spray a non stick frying pan with low fat cooking spray. Fry the chopped onion with the pepper and the rest of the ginger for 4 minutes until caramelised.

❸ Tip three quarters of the beans and the egg into a food processor. Whiz to a paste then transfer to a bowl. Stir the curry powder into the pepper and onions and cook for a few seconds, then tip this into the bowl, along with the rest of the beans and season. Bring together by hand and shape into eight cakes.

❹ Rinse the frying pan, return to the heat and spray with low fat cooking spray. Fry the bean cakes for 3 minutes on each side until golden brown and crusty. Serve with the onion relish.

Salmon with couscous crust

Takes 25 minutes
23 *POINTS* values per recipe
346 calories per serving
Serves 4

grated zest and juice of a lemon
4 x 125 g (4½ oz) skinless salmon fillets
110 g (4 oz) plain couscous
150 ml (5 fl oz) hot vegetable stock
3 tablespoons chopped fresh parsley
1 egg, beaten
350 g (12 oz) green beans, trimmed
low fat cooking spray
3 ripe tomatoes, diced

❶ Preheat the oven to Gas Mark 6/200°C/fan oven 180°C. Place the salmon on a plate and drizzle over half of the lemon juice.

❷ Place the couscous in a bowl, pour in the hot stock, stir once, cover, and leave to stand for 5 minutes. Add 2 tablespoons of parsley, lemon zest and the remaining lemon juice. Tip the couscous out on to a plate.

❸ Shake the excess lemon juice from the salmon, then dip each fillet first in the beaten egg, then press into the couscous to coat thickly on all sides. Transfer to a baking tray and bake for 15 minutes until crisp and golden.

❹ Meanwhile, cook the green beans in boiling water for 5 minutes. Drain. Rinse the saucepan and then spray with low fat cooking spray, add the tomatoes and cook for 2 minutes over a fairly high heat, until softened and forming a sauce. Toss the beans with the tomatoes, adding the rest of the parsley.

❺ Serve the salmon on a bed of saucy beans.

Middle Eastern meatballs

❄ Takes 15 minutes to prepare, 15 minutes to cook
28 *POINTS* values per recipe
375 calories per serving
Serves 4

Meatballs are always a popular family meal, but the flavour in this recipe has a real twist. Spoon the meatballs on to a bed of cooked couscous (150 g/5½ oz) per person, for an additional 2½ *POINTS* values per serving, for the ideal accompaniment.

low fat cooking spray
1 onion, half chopped and half grated
300 ml (10 fl oz) vegetable stock
2 wholewheat crispbreads, crumbled
500 g (1 lb 2 oz) lean minced lamb
½ x 25 g packet fresh coriander, stalks chopped and
**   leaves reserved**
1 teaspoon ground cinnamon
1 teaspoon ground cumin
1 x 400 g can chopped tomatoes
1 x 410 g can chick peas, rinsed and drained
salt and freshly ground black pepper

❶ Spray a lidded flameproof casserole with low fat cooking spray. Fry the chopped half of the onion for 2 minutes. Add 3 tablespoons of stock, cover and cook for 2 minutes more.

❷ Place the grated onion in a mixing bowl, stir in the crispbread crumbs and 2 tablespoons of stock to moisten them. Add the lamb mince, coriander stalks, half a teaspoon of the ground cinnamon and season. Mix well, then shape into 20 meatballs.

❸ Add the cumin, the remaining half teaspoon of cinnamon, tomatoes, chick peas and the rest of the stock to the casserole and simmer for 5 minutes.

❹ Meanwhile, spray a non stick frying pan with low fat cooking spray and brown the meatballs for 5 minutes, turning to colour them evenly. Gently stir the browned meatballs into the sauce and simmer, uncovered, for 15 minutes. Serve with the coriander leaves scattered over the top.

These quick and easy meatballs are defintely worth staying in for.

Roast chicken ratatouille

Takes 10 minutes to prepare, 30 minutes to cook
9½ *POINTS* values per recipe
216 calories per serving
Serves 4

Serve with a medium (225 g/8 oz) jacket potato per person, for an additional 2½ *POINTS* values per serving.

3 mixed peppers, de-seeded and chopped roughly
1 courgette, chopped roughly
1 aubergine, chopped roughly
2 garlic cloves, crushed
1 teaspoon plus a pinch of dried mixed herbs
low fat cooking spray
4 x 150 g (5½ oz) skinless boneless chicken breasts
1 x 400 g can chopped tomatoes

❶ Preheat the oven to Gas Mark 6/200°C/fan oven 180°C. In a large roasting tin, toss together the peppers, courgette and aubergine with the garlic. Add 1 teaspoon of herbs and coat with low fat cooking spray. Spread out in a shallow layer, then pop in the oven for 15 minutes.

❷ After 15 minutes, stir the vegetables around and push to one side of the tin. Sprinkle the chicken breasts with the pinch of dried mixed herbs and place in the space in the roasting tin. Return to the oven for 15 minutes.

❸ Lastly, mix in the chopped tomatoes with the roasted vegetables and return to the oven for a final 5 minutes. Serve the chicken on top of the ratatouille.

Ⓨ **Tip** For a vegetarian version, use 8 x 52 g Quorn Chicken Style Fillets instead of the chicken breasts, for a *POINTS* value of 1½ per serving.

Grilled tropical fruits

Takes 20 minutes
7½ *POINTS* values per recipe
96 calories per serving
Serves 4

Caramelising really brings out the full flavour of the fruit, while a touch of ginger adds a gentle kick of heat.

1 large ripe mango
1 ripe papaya
½ fresh pineapple
½ teaspoon ground ginger
150 g (5½ oz) 0% fat Greek yogurt
grated zest and juice of a lime

❶ Preheat the grill to its highest setting.
❷ Peel the mango and papaya using a vegetable peeler. Cut the cheeks off each side of the flat stone in the centre of the mango, then slice each cheek into four wedges. Halve the papaya, scoop out the seeds and cut each half into four wedges.
❸ Cut the pineapple into eight long wedges, slice out the core and then cut the flesh away from the skin.
❹ Place all the fruit wedges on a grill tray and sprinkle with the ginger. Grill for 8–10 minutes until lightly caramelised. Meanwhile, trim any remaining mango flesh from the stone and chop finely. Mix into the yogurt, followed by the lime zest.
❺ Squeeze the lime juice over the grilled fruit, then serve piled on to plates, topped with the zesty yogurt.

Very berry ice

❄ **Takes 15 minutes + 3½ hours freezing + softening**
3 *POINTS* values per recipe
88 calories per serving
Serves 4

If you want to make this recipe even easier, once the yogurt has been mixed in, skip the whisking of the frozen mixture and pour it into eight lolly moulds, then freeze until firm. Dip the moulds into hot water to release the lollies.

1 x 12 g sachet sugar free raspberry jelly
300 ml (10 fl oz) boiling water
350 g (12 oz) mixed summer berries, e.g. raspberries, strawberries, blackcurrants
200 g (7 oz) low fat vanilla flavour yogurt

❶ In a measuring jug, sprinkle the jelly crystals over the boiling water and stir to dissolve, then make it up to 600 ml (1 pint) with cold water.
❷ In a blender or with a hand blender, whiz the fruits to a purée then mix with the jelly. Pour into a shallow tray or plastic box, cover and place in the freezer for 1½ hours, until beginning to freeze around the edges. Whisk the mixture, making sure that you mix in the frozen bits from around the edge of the container. Mix in the vanilla yogurt until smooth, then return the mixture to the freezer.
❸ Whisk the mixture twice more, at intervals of roughly 1 hour. The whisking process breaks up large ice crystals, so that you get a smoother textured ice.
❹ Once the ice is firm, serve in scoops. If the ice has been left to freeze completely solid, it will need to soften in the fridge for 30 minutes or so before scooping, or it can be softened on defrost in the microwave, in blasts of 30 seconds, until ready.

Iced banoffee sundae

Ⓨ **Takes 5 minutes + 1½ –2 hours freezing**
10 *POINTS* values per recipe
156 calories per serving
Serves 4

Freezing slices of banana gives them a fabulous texture rather like ice cream, which is the inspiration for this sweet and fruity sundae.

4 small bananas, sliced thickly
400 g (14 oz) smooth low fat toffee flavour yogurt e.g. Weight Watchers or Müllerlight
250 g (9 oz) fresh raspberries
100 g (3½ oz) low fat plain fromage frais

❶ Line a baking tray with clingfilm. Spread the bananas out on the tray in a single layer. Cover with more clingfilm and freeze for 1½ –2 hours or until firm.
❷ For each sundae, spoon some toffee yogurt into a tall glass and then add some raspberries and frozen banana slices. Repeat the layers again and then finish with the fromage frais. Serve immediately.

Frozen bananas with toffee and raspberries are devilishly delicious.

fabulous

Planning your week ahead: Chapter four

Dairy
- Crème fraîche, half fat, 2 tbsp
- Eggs, 2
- Filo pastry, frozen, 1 x 270 g packet (6 sheets)
- Goat's cheese, mild soft, 150 g
- Low fat soft cheese, 50 g
- Milk, skimmed, 1100 ml
- Parmesan cheese, 20 g
- Yogurt, low fat, natural, 225 g

Dry and canned ingredients
- Almonds, flaked, 15 g
- Bread, white or wholemeal, 2 slices
- Caster sugar, 175 g
- Cocoa powder, 25 g
- Passata, 1 x 700 g jar
- Penne, dried, 175 g

- Pittas, medium, 4
- Sultanas, 25 g
- Yeast, fast action, 1 packet

Fruit, vegetables and herbs
- Bananas, 2
- Butternut squash, large, 1 x 800 g
- Carrots, 500 g
- Chives, fresh, 1 x 25 g packet
- Cooking apples, 450 g
- Cucumber, 50 g
- Iceberg lettuce, 75 g
- Leeks, 3
- Lemon, 1 large
- Mushrooms, small dark gilled, 300 g
- Orange, 1
- Parsnips, 400 g
- Passion fruit, 2
- Peas, frozen, 200 g

- Potatoes, 275 g
- Red onion, 1
- Savoy cabbage, 1
- Thyme, fresh, 1 x 25 g packet
- Vegetables, mixed frozen (carrots, green beans, peas and sweetcorn), 150 g

Meat and fish
- Bacon, lean back, 2 rashers
- Beef mince, lean, 450 g
- Chicken breasts, skinless and boneless, 4 x 150 g
- Lamb leg steaks, lean, 300 g
- Parma ham, 4 slices
- Pork fillet, lean, 500 g
- Trout fillets, 4 x 110 g

And from your Kitchen Basics, you will need the following ingredients: black peppercorns, chicken stock cubes, chilli powder, cornflour, curry powder, dried mixed herbs, garlic, ground cinnamon, ground cumin, low fat cooking spray, low fat polyunsaturated margarine, mint sauce, olive oil, plain flour, salt, self raising flour, vanilla extract and vegetable stock cubes.

Creamy carrot and orange soup

Y ❄ Takes 10 minutes to prepare, 15 minutes to cook

7½ *POINTS* values per recipe

137 calories per serving

Serves 4

A hint of orange brings out the natural sweetness of the root vegetables in this heart-warming soup.

1.2 litres (2 pints) vegetable stock
500 g (1 lb 2 oz) carrots, peeled and grated coarsely
400 g (14 oz) parsnips, peeled and grated coarsely
finely grated zest and juice of an orange
2 tablespoons half fat crème fraîche
salt and freshly ground black pepper

❶ In a large lidded saucepan, bring the stock to the boil. Add the grated vegetables, orange zest and juice. Season to taste.
❷ Cover and simmer for 15 minutes until the vegetables are tender.
❸ In a blender or with a hand blender, blend the soup and crème fraîche together until smooth, then serve in warmed bowls.

Spicy samosas

Y ❄ (samosas only, before cooking)

Takes 20 minutes to prepare, 15 minutes to cook

12 *POINTS* values per recipe

165 calories per serving

Serves 4, makes 8 samosas

275 g (9½ oz) potatoes, peeled and diced
150 g (5½ oz) frozen mixed vegetables (e.g. carrots, green beans, peas and sweetcorn)
low fat cooking spray
1½ teaspoons curry powder
4 x 45 g sheets of filo such as Jus Rol (from a 270 g packet of 6 sheets, reserving or freezing 2 sheets for the Apple and sultana filo tarts on page 62)
2 teaspoons mint sauce
150 g (5½ oz) low fat natural yogurt

❶ Preheat the oven to Gas Mark 6/200ºC/fan oven 180ºC. Bring a lidded saucepan of water to the boil and add the potatoes. Cover and cook for 4 minutes. Add the vegetables, replace the lid and cook for 3 minutes more. Drain the potatoes and vegetables in a colander.
❷ Spray the saucepan with low fat cooking spray. Return the vegetables to the pan, mix in the curry powder and cook, stirring, for 1 minute. Tip on to a plate to cool.
❸ Cut each sheet of filo in half lengthways to give eight long strips. Working with one strip at a time, spray with low fat cooking spray and spoon one eighth of the filling on the top. Bring the top left corner across to the other side to make a triangle. Flip this over and over until you reach the bottom of the strip and the filling is completely enclosed. Place on a baking tray and spray with low fat cooking spray. Repeat to make eight samosas in total.
❹ Bake for 15 minutes until crisp and golden brown.
❺ Stir the mint sauce into the yogurt and serve the sauce with two samosas per person.

These crisp, curried samosas can be served straight from the oven, or at room temperature in a lunchbox.

Chilli lamb pittas

Takes 10 minutes
17 *POINTS* values per recipe
225 calories per serving
Serves 4

You can adjust the spiciness of this recipe to suit your palate by using more or less chilli powder. With a cooling cucumber and yogurt relish to temper the heat, these pittas are a great alternative to a kebab.

½ teaspoon ground cumin
¼ teaspoon chilli powder
300 g (10½ oz) lean lamb leg steaks
low fat cooking spray
50 g (1¾ oz) cucumber, diced
75 g (2¾ oz) low fat natural yogurt
4 medium pittas
75 g (2¾ oz) Iceberg lettuce, shredded
salt and freshly ground black pepper

❶ Mix the cumin and chilli powder together with some seasoning, then rub this spice mixture into the lamb steaks. Heat a non stick frying pan, spray with low fat cooking spray and pan fry the lamb steaks for 3–4 minutes on each side until cooked to your liking.
❷ Meanwhile, mix the cucumber into the yogurt to make the relish, and season to taste.
❸ Under a medium grill, lightly toast the pittas then cut each one in half to make two pockets. Stuff with shredded lettuce and spoon in the cucumber relish. Slice the lamb into strips and pile into the pitta pockets. Serve immediately.

Almond crusted trout

Takes 20 minutes
17½ POINTS values per recipe
182 calories per serving
Serves 4

Serve with a medium portion (100 g/3½ oz) of boiled new potatoes per person, for an additional **POINTS** value of 1 per serving.

2 medium slices white or wholemeal bread (35 g each), torn into small pieces
15 g (½ oz) low fat polyunsaturated margarine, melted
15 g (½ oz) flaked almonds
4 x 110 g (4 oz) trout fillets
low fat cooking spray
1 red onion, sliced thinly
2 rashers lean back bacon, diced
2 garlic cloves, crushed
1 Savoy cabbage, shredded
salt and freshly ground black pepper

❶ Preheat the grill to a medium setting.

❷ In a blender or with a hand blender, whiz the bread to crumbs. Mix together with the melted margarine and the almonds.

❸ Lay out the trout fillets on a grill pan, flesh side up, and season lightly. Press the almond crumb crust on to the trout.

❹ Spray a large non stick frying pan or wok with low fat cooking spray. Stir fry the onion for 3 minutes over a medium heat to soften. Add the bacon and garlic and cook for 2 minutes until lightly browned. Add the cabbage and 4 tablespoons of water. Stir fry for 5 minutes until wilted and tender.

❺ While the cabbage is cooking, grill the trout for 5–6 minutes until it is cooked through and has a crisp golden crust (there is no need to turn over the fish during cooking). Serve the trout with the sautéed cabbage.

Cheesy chicken with butternut chips

Takes 10 minutes to prepare, 30 minutes to cook
16½ *POINTS* values per recipe
295 calories per serving
Serves 4

Soft goat's cheese has a mild tangy flavour, but if you prefer, you can use the same amount of low fat soft cheese with herbs instead, for a **POINTS** value of 3½ per serving.

1 x 800 g (1 lb 11 oz) butternut squash, peeled and
    de-seeded
low fat cooking spray
75 g (2¾ oz) mild soft goat's cheese
1 tablespoon snipped fresh chives
4 x 150 g (5½ oz) skinless boneless chicken breasts
4 slices Parma ham
freshly ground black pepper

❶ Preheat the oven to Gas Mark 6/200°C/fan oven 180°C.
❷ Cut the squash into finger width chips. Spread out on a large baking tray, and lightly coat with low fat cooking spray. Season with freshly ground black pepper, then roast in the oven for 10 minutes.
❸ In a bowl, mix the goat's cheese with the chives. Cut a pocket in the thickest part of each chicken breast and spoon in the cheese mixture. Tuck a slice of Parma ham over each chicken breast, covering up the pocket of stuffing.
❹ Remove the baking tray from the oven, add the chicken breasts to the tray, stirring the butternut squash chips around. Cook in the oven for a further 20 minutes, until the chicken is cooked through and the chips are tender and beginning to brown.

Pasticcio

❄ (before cooking)
Takes 25 minutes to prepare, 20 minutes to cook
29½ *POINTS* values per recipe
425 calories per serving
Serves 4

450 g (1 lb) lean minced beef
3 garlic cloves, crushed
2 teaspoons dried mixed herbs
600 g (1 lb 5 oz) passata
175 g (6 oz) dried penne
25 g (1 oz) cornflour
425 ml (15 fl oz) skimmed milk
20 g (¾ oz) freshly grated Parmesan cheese
salt and freshly ground black pepper

❶ Preheat the oven to Gas Mark 6/200°C/fan oven 180°C. In a lidded non stick saucepan, dry fry the mince for 5 minutes, stirring to break up the meat. Add the garlic and herbs and cook for 1 minute. Pour in the passata, season, cover and simmer for 15 minutes.
❷ Meanwhile, bring a saucepan of water to the boil and cook the pasta for 10 minutes or according to the packet instructions until tender.
❸ To make a white sauce, blend the cornflour with a little of the milk in a non stick pan to make a smooth paste, then mix in the rest of the milk. Bring to the boil, stirring until thickened, then simmer for 2 minutes.
❹ Drain the pasta and mix with the meat sauce. Tip into a baking dish and pour the white sauce on top. Scatter with Parmesan cheese.
❺ Bake for 20 minutes until the top is golden brown.

Ⓥ **Tip** For a vegetarian version, replace the minced beef with the same quantity of Quorn mince, for a *POINTS* value of 5 per serving.

Serve with a crisp mixed salad of crunchy shredded Iceberg lettuce, coarsely grated carrot and chunks of fresh tomato, for no additional *POINTS* values.

7½ POINTS VALUE

Garlic mushroom and goat's cheese pizza

🅨 Takes 15 minutes to prepare + 1 hour 10 minutes rising, 15 minutes to cook

20½ *POINTS* values per recipe

341 calories per serving

Serves 4

Serve with a mixed zero *POINTS* value salad, dressed with a little balsamic vinegar.

300 g (10½ oz) plain flour, 3 teaspoons reserved

2 teaspoons fast action yeast

1 teaspoon salt

2 teaspoons olive oil

low fat cooking spray

300 g (10½ oz) small dark gilled mushrooms, halved

2 garlic cloves, crushed

100 g (3½ oz) passata

1 tablespoon fresh thyme leaves

75 g (2¾ oz) mild soft goat's cheese

freshly ground black pepper

❶ Sift the flour into a mixing bowl. Stir in the yeast and salt. Make a well in the centre and add the olive oil. Mix in about 200 ml (7 fl oz) warm water, or just enough to bring the mixture together to form a soft, but not sticky, dough.

❷ Dust the counter surface with 2 teaspoons of the reserved flour and turn out the dough on to the floured surface. Knead for 3 minutes until smooth. Return to the bowl, cover with clingfilm and leave to rise in a warm place for 1 hour, or until doubled in size.

❸ Preheat the oven to Gas Mark 7/220°C/fan oven 200°C. Spray a lidded non stick saucepan with low fat cooking spray. Add the mushrooms, garlic and 1 tablespoon of water. Season with freshly ground black pepper. Cover and cook for 3–4 minutes until juicy. Cook for a further 1–2 minutes with the lid off to evaporate the juices, then leave to cool.

❹ Dust the counter surface with the remaining 1 teaspoon of flour and roll out the pizza base to fit a 20 x 30 cm (8 x 12 inch) baking tray. Transfer the rolled base to the baking tray.

❺ Spread the base with the passata and scatter on half the thyme. Top with the mushrooms and dot with small clumps of the goat's cheese.

❻ Leave to rise for 10 minutes, then bake for 15 minutes until well risen and crisp. Scatter with the remaining thyme just before serving and cut into quarters.

Quick roast pork fillet

Takes 35 minutes
18 *POINTS* values per recipe
273 calories per serving
Serves 4

Serve with 200 g (7 oz) potatoes (mashed with 2 tablespoons of skimmed milk) per person for an extra *POINTS* value of 2½ per serving.

3 garlic cloves, crushed
3 tablespoons snipped fresh chives
3 tablespoons chopped fresh thyme
500 g (1 lb 2 oz) lean pork fillet
15 g (½ oz) low fat polyunsaturated margarine
3 leeks, trimmed and sliced
150 ml (5 fl oz) chicken stock
200 g (7 oz) frozen peas
50 g (1¾ oz) low fat soft cheese
freshly ground black pepper

❶ Preheat the oven to Gas Mark 6/200°C/fan oven 180°C. Mix together two crushed garlic cloves with the chives and half the thyme. Roll the pork fillet in the garlic and herb mixture to coat. Place on a roasting tray and roast in the oven for 25 minutes until cooked through but still juicy – the juices should run clear when the thickest part of the pork is pierced with a sharp knife or skewer.

❷ After the pork has been cooking for 15 minutes, melt the margarine in a lidded non stick saucepan. Stir in the leeks, the remaining garlic and 3 tablespoons of stock. Cover the pan and cook for 3 minutes. Pour in the rest of the stock, add the peas and cook, covered, for a further 5 minutes.

❸ Mix the soft cheese and remaining thyme into the leeks and peas. Season with freshly ground black pepper and serve with the pork, carved into thick slices.

Chocolate banana custards

Takes 10 minutes + 1 hour chilling
11 *POINTS* values per recipe
201 calories per serving
Serves 4

A gorgeous dessert.

60 g (2 oz) caster sugar
25 g (1 oz) cocoa powder
25 g (1 oz) cornflour
425 ml (15 fl oz) skimmed milk
2 teaspoons vanilla extract
2 bananas, sliced

1 To make a chocolate custard, mix the caster sugar, cocoa powder and cornflour together in a non stick saucepan. Add a little of the milk to blend the mixture to a paste, then stir in the rest of the milk until smooth.
2 Heat the mixture, stirring, until it comes to the boil then lower the heat and simmer for 3 minutes. Remove from the heat and stir in the vanilla extract.
3 Divide the bananas between four small dishes or glasses then pour the chocolate custard on top. Press clingfilm on to the surface of each one to stop a skin forming. Once cool, chill in the fridge for 1 hour or until ready to serve.

Apple and sultana filo tarts

Vegan
Takes 20 minutes
8 *POINTS* values per recipe
164 calories per serving
Serves 4

These individual apple tarts are terrific served with 150 g (5½ oz) low fat custard per person, for an additional ***POINTS*** value of 2 per serving.

2 x 45 g sheets filo pastry such as Jus Rol (from a 270 g
  packet of 6 sheets, reserving or freezing 4 sheets for
  the Spicy samosas on page 52)
low fat cooking spray
450 g (1 lb) cooking apples, peeled, cored and diced
40 g (1½ oz) caster sugar
25 g (1 oz) sultanas
¼ teaspoon ground cinnamon

❶ Preheat the oven to Gas Mark 5/190ºC/fan oven 170ºC.
❷ Spray the first sheet of filo with low fat cooking spray, then layer the second sheet on top and lightly spray that too. Cut into two long strips, then cut each strip into four squares. Layer up two squares for each tart, laying them at an angle so that the corners form a star shape. Spray four holes of a non stick muffin tin with low fat cooking spray and press in the filo stacks. Bake for 6 minutes until golden and crisp.
❸ Meanwhile, mix the apples with the sugar, sultanas and cinnamon in a lidded saucepan. Add 1 tablespoon of water, cover the pan and cook for 6 minutes until the apples are collapsed and fluffy.
❹ Spoon the apple filling into the tart cases and return to the oven for 3 minutes. Serve warm.

Lemon and passion fruit pudding

Takes 10 minutes to prepare, 30 minutes to cook
14 *POINTS* values per recipe
231 calories per serving
Serves 4

low fat cooking spray
50 g (1¾ oz) low fat polyunsaturated margarine
75 g (2¾ oz) caster sugar
2 eggs, separated
grated zest and juice of a large lemon
50 g (1¾ oz) self raising flour, sifted
250 ml (9 fl oz) skimmed milk
2 passion fruit, halved

❶ Preheat the oven to Gas Mark 4/180ºC/fan oven 160ºC. Spray a baking dish, measuring about 15 x 20 cm (6 x 8 inches), with low fat cooking spray.
❷ In a bowl, using an electric mixer, beat the margarine, sugar, egg yolks and lemon zest together for 1 minute until pale. Whisk in the flour, followed by the lemon juice and then the milk to give a thin batter.
❸ Clean the whisk beaters. In a separate clean bowl, whisk the egg whites to soft peaks. Gently fold the egg whites into the batter, then pour the foamy mixture into the baking dish. Spoon the passion fruit seeds randomly over the pudding.
❹ Bake on the centre shelf for 30 minutes until golden brown and firm in the centre.

satisfying

Planning your week ahead: Chapter five

Dairy
- Blue cheese, 100 g
- Cheddar cheese, reduced fat, 60 g
- Crème fraîche, half fat, 4 tbsp
- Eggs, 7
- Ice cream, low fat vanilla, 4 scoops (240 g)
- Low fat soft cheese with garlic and herbs, 75 g
- Milk, skimmed, 555 ml
- Parmesan cheese, 70 g
- Yogurt, Greek, 0 % fat, 75 g
- Yogurt, low fat, natural, 250 g
- Yogurt, low fat, vanilla flavour, 200 g

Dried and canned ingredients
- Bagels, medium, 4
- Bread, white or wholemeal (75 g breadcrumbs, 100 g diced)
- Caster sugar, 42 g
- Haricot beans, 2 x 410 g cans
- Honey, 70 ml
- Penne, dried, 175 g
- Pine nut kernels, 15 g
- Puy lentils, dried, 150 g
- Rosemary, dried, ½ tsp
- Soft light brown sugar, 85 g
- Tomatoes, chopped, 1 x 400 g can
- Tuna in brine, 1 x 200 g can
- White chocolate, 50 g

Fruit, vegetables and herbs (fresh and frozen)
- Apple, 1
- Asparagus, thin, 200 g
- Baby Chantenay carrots, 500 g
- Bananas, 4
- Blueberries, frozen, 350 g
- Cherry tomatoes, 250 g
- Cranberries, frozen, 100 g
- Lemon, 1
- Lime, 1
- Mint, fresh, 1 x 25 g packet
- Orange, 1
- Peas, frozen, 200 g
- Potatoes, 1.1 kg
- Root ginger, fresh, a small knob (for 1 tbsp)
- Spinach, young leaf, 75 g
- Spring onions, 5 bunches
- Sweet potatoes, 750 g
- Thyme, fresh, 1 x 25 g packet
- Tomatoes, 4
- Watercress, 1 x 85 g packet

Meat and fish
- Beef medallion steaks, lean, 4 x 110 g
- Lamb leg steaks, lean, 400 g
- Pork loin steaks, lean, 4 x 150 g
- Turkey breast steaks, 4 x 125 g

And from your Kitchen Basics, you will need the following ingredients: apple sauce, black peppercorns, cornflour, cumin seeds, dried mixed herbs, garlic, gelatine, ground cinnamon, ground mixed spice, low fat cooking spray, low fat polyunsaturated margarine, onions, plain flour, porridge oats, salt and vegetable stock cubes.

Asparagus pasta salad with blue cheese dressing

Takes 15 minutes
16½ *POINTS* values per recipe
267 calories per serving
Serves 4

The punchy flavour of blue cheese makes a rich tasting dressing, but without having too many *POINTS* values. You only need a small amount to give a lot of flavour.

175 g (6 oz) dried penne
200 g (7 oz) thin asparagus, chopped roughly
15 g (½ oz) pine nut kernels
50 g (1¾ oz) blue cheese, crumbled
100 g (3½ oz) low fat natural yogurt
75 g (2¾ oz) young leaf spinach
freshly ground black pepper

❶ Bring a saucepan of water to the boil and cook the pasta for 10–12 minutes or according to the packet instructions until tender, adding the asparagus for the last 3 minutes of the cooking time.
❷ Meanwhile, in a non stick frying pan, dry fry the pine nut kernels for 1–2 minutes, shaking until golden brown. Set aside.
❸ In a mixing bowl, crumble the blue cheese, mash with a fork and gradually mix in the yogurt to make the dressing. Season to taste with freshly ground black pepper.
❹ Drain the pasta and asparagus and rinse in cold water. Tip into the mixing bowl and toss with the blue cheese dressing to coat, mixing in the spinach leaves at the same time. Serve scattered with the toasted pine nut kernels.

Lunchbox pea and mint frittatas

Takes 8 minutes to prepare, 12 minutes to cook + cooling
11 *POINTS* values per recipe
153 calories per serving
Serves 4

These are best when served at room temperature, rather than piping hot or fridge cold. Serve with a mixture of tender salad leaves, for no additional *POINTS* values.

low fat cooking spray
200 g (7 oz) frozen peas
3 eggs plus 2 egg whites
2 tablespoons half fat crème fraîche
2 tablespoons skimmed milk
2 tablespoons chopped fresh mint
15 g (½ oz) freshly grated Parmesan cheese
salt and freshly ground black pepper

❶ Preheat the oven to Gas Mark 4/180°C/fan oven 160°C. Lightly spray eight holes of a non stick muffin tin with low fat cooking spray.
❷ Bring a saucepan of water to the boil. Add the peas, bring back to the boil and then drain the peas immediately. Divide between the greased muffin tin holes.
❸ In a bowl, beat the eggs and egg whites with the crème fraîche and milk. Season and then stir in the mint and Parmesan cheese. Pour on top of the peas.
❹ Bake the frittatas in the oven for 12 minutes until firm, puffy and lightly golden.
❺ Remove from the tin and leave to cool slightly before serving each person with two.

These yummy little frittatas are the perfect size for a packed lunch or picnic.

Watercress and blue cheese soup

Takes 20 minutes
10½ *POINTS* values per recipe
152 calories per serving
Serves 4

A little blue cheese goes a long way in this recipe, with the nuggets of cheese melting lusciously into the soup and boosting the flavour.

25 g (1 oz) low fat polyunsaturated margarine
2 bunches spring onions, chopped
300 g (10½ oz) potatoes, peeled and grated coarsely
850 ml (1½ pints) vegetable stock
1 x 85 g packet watercress
salt and freshly ground black pepper
50 g (1¾ oz) blue cheese, crumbled, to serve

❶ In a large lidded non stick saucepan, melt the margarine, add the spring onions and cook for 2 minutes until softened.
❷ Add the potatoes and stock. Cover the pan and bring to the boil. Cook for 6–8 minutes until the potato is tender.
❸ Stir the watercress into the soup, then transfer to a blender or using a hand blender, blend until smooth. Check the seasoning and then ladle the soup into warm bowls. Scatter the blue cheese over each bowl, to melt as you eat it.

Tuna melt bagels

Takes 15 minutes
19½ *POINTS* values per recipe
342 calories per serving
Serves 4

An American classic which is ideal served with a crisp mixed zero *POINTS* value salad.

4 medium bagels, split
1 x 200 g can tuna in brine, drained
4 spring onions, chopped
75 g (2¾ oz) 0% fat Greek yogurt
60 g (2 oz) reduced fat Cheddar cheese, grated
4 tomatoes, sliced
freshly ground black pepper

❶ Preheat the grill to medium high and lightly toast the bagels on both sides.
❷ Meanwhile, in a bowl, flake in the tuna and mix with the spring onions, yogurt and cheese. Season to taste with freshly ground black pepper.
❸ Divide up the tomato slices and place on top of the cut sides of the bagels. Spoon the tuna mixture on top. Grill for 3–4 minutes until golden and bubbling, then serve immediately.

Lamb and haricot bean fricassee

❄ **Takes 15 minutes**
19 *POINTS* values per recipe
266 calories per serving
Serves 4

Deeply savoury, this hearty fricassee needs only a simple zero *POINTS* value green vegetable such as cabbage to accompany it.

400 g (14 oz) lean lamb leg steaks, diced
low fat cooking spray
2 bunches spring onions, cut into chunky pieces
2 garlic cloves, crushed
½ teaspoon dried rosemary
150 ml (5 fl oz) vegetable stock
2 x 410 g cans haricot beans, rinsed and drained
2 tablespoons half fat crème fraîche
salt and freshly ground black pepper

❶ Season the lamb then spray a large non stick frying pan with low fat cooking spray and brown the meat, over a high heat, for 4–5 minutes.
❷ Add the spring onions, garlic and rosemary to the frying pan. Cook for 1 minute more, stirring.
❸ Mix in the stock and haricot beans then simmer for 3 minutes. Stir in the crème fraîche to make a sauce, check the seasoning and serve.

Crispy Parmesan turkey with roast tomatoes

Takes 25 minutes
17 *POINTS* values per recipe
279 calories per serving
Serves 4

Serve with a medium portion (150 g/5½ oz) of cooked spaghetti per person, for a classic Italian combination and an extra 2 *POINTS* values per serving.

75 g (2¾ oz) fresh white or wholemeal breadcrumbs
40 g (1½ oz) freshly grated Parmesan cheese
4 x 125 g (4½ oz) turkey breast steaks
1 egg, beaten
low fat cooking spray
250 g (9 oz) cherry tomatoes, halved
½ teaspoon caster sugar
1 tablespoon fresh thyme leaves
salt and freshly ground black pepper

❶ Preheat the oven to Gas Mark 6/200°C/fan oven 180°C and place a baking tray in the oven to heat.
❷ Mix the breadcrumbs and Parmesan cheese together on a plate. Dip the turkey breast steaks, first in beaten egg, then press into the crumb mixture to coat.
❸ Remove the baking tray from the oven and place the coated turkey steaks on it. Spray with low fat cooking spray and then place the tray on the top shelf of the oven to cook for 10 minutes.
❹ Meanwhile, spread the cherry tomatoes out in a roasting tin, cut side up. Sprinkle with the sugar and thyme. Season then spray lightly with low fat cooking spray. Add the roasting tin to the oven and cook below the turkey for 10 minutes. Serve the turkey with the tomatoes on the side.

Puy lentil pie

Y ❄ **Takes 25 minutes to prepare, 20 minutes to cook**
19 *POINTS* values per recipe
338 calories per serving
Serves 4

Great for a chilly day, or for when you're feeling particularly hungry. Serve with runner beans or broccoli, for no additional *POINTS* values.

150 g (5½ oz) dried Puy lentils
800 g (1 lb 11 oz) potatoes, peeled and chopped roughly
low fat cooking spray
1 onion, chopped finely
1 x 400 g can chopped tomatoes
1 teaspoon dried mixed herbs
75 g (2¾ oz) low fat soft cheese with garlic and herbs
5 tablespoons skimmed milk
15 g (½ oz) freshly grated Parmesan cheese
freshly ground black pepper

❶ Preheat the oven to Gas Mark 6/200°C/fan oven 180°C. Bring a saucepan of water to the boil and cook the lentils for 20 minutes or until tender.

❷ Bring another saucepan of water to the boil, add the potatoes and boil for 12–15 minutes until tender.

❸ While the lentils and potatoes are cooking, spray a non stick frying pan with low fat cooking spray and cook the onion for 4 minutes until slightly softened. Add the tomatoes and dried herbs and season with freshly ground black pepper to taste. Simmer for about 8 minutes.

❹ Drain the potatoes and mash with the soft cheese and milk.

❺ Drain the lentils and stir together with the tomato sauce, then tip into a baking dish. Spoon the mash over the top and scatter with Parmesan cheese. Bake for 20 minutes until golden brown and serve.

Gingered beef
with sweet potato mash

Takes 25 minutes

19½ *POINTS* values per recipe

366 calories per serving

Serves 4

Sweet potato mash makes a nice change and has a luxurious velvety texture. Serve with sugar snap peas, for no extra ***POINTS*** values.

750 g (1 lb 10 oz) sweet potatoes, peeled and diced roughly

1 tablespoon freshly grated root ginger

2 heaped teaspoons honey

finely grated zest and juice of ½ a lime

4 x 110 g (4 oz) lean beef medallion steaks

low fat cooking spray

2 teaspoons low fat polyunsaturated margarine

salt and freshly ground black pepper

❶ Bring a saucepan of water to the boil and cook the sweet potatoes for 12–15 minutes until tender.

❷ Meanwhile, make a paste from half the ginger, the honey, lime zest and juice. Spread over the steaks on both sides and set aside for 5–10 minutes.

❸ Spray a non stick frying pan with low fat cooking spray and pan fry the steaks for 2–3 minutes on each side, or until cooked to your liking.

❹ Drain the sweet potatoes in a colander. Melt the margarine in the saucepan, add the remaining ginger and cook for 30 seconds until aromatic. Return the potatoes to the pan and mash with the ginger. Season to taste and serve with the beef steaks.

Pork steaks with honey and cumin roasted carrots

Takes 35 minutes

14½ *POINTS* values per recipe

396 calories per serving

Serves 4

A mouth watering combination of tender pork and sticky caramelised carrots. This is lovely served with a medium portion (150 g/5½ oz) of cooked rice per person, for an additional ***POINTS*** value of 3 per serving.

500 g (1 lb 2 oz) baby Chantenay carrots

low fat cooking spray

grated zest and juice of a lemon

4 x 150 g (5½ oz) lean pork loin steaks

2 tablespoons honey

1 tablespoon cumin seeds

freshly ground black pepper

❶ Preheat the oven to Gas Mark 6/200°C/fan oven 180°C.

❷ Toss the carrots with freshly ground black pepper and spray with low fat cooking spray. Spread out on a large foil lined roasting tray. Place in the oven for 20 minutes.

❸ Meanwhile, press the lemon zest on to the pork steaks. Mix 2 teaspoons of lemon juice with the honey and cumin seeds and set aside.

❹ When the carrots have had about 15 minutes in the oven, heat a non stick frying pan on the hob. Spray with low fat cooking spray then brown the pork steaks for 1 minute on each side. Pour in the rest of the lemon juice and bubble briefly, then remove from the heat.

❺ Transfer the pork steaks to the tray alongside the carrots, spooning the cooking juices over the meat. Pour the honey mixture over the carrots and toss to coat.

❻ Return to the oven and cook for 5 minutes, then stir the carrots again and cook for a final 5 minutes until sticky and caramelised and the pork steaks are cooked.

Cinnamon bananas

Y Takes 5 minutes

13½ *POINTS* values per recipe

256 calories per serving

Serves 4

This fabulous speedy pud is a great mixture of hot and cold elements.

4 teaspoons low fat polyunsaturated margarine
2 tablespoons honey
¼ teaspoon ground cinnamon
4 bananas, sliced thickly
juice of an orange
4 x 60 g (2 oz) scoops low fat vanilla ice cream

❶ In a non stick frying pan, melt the margarine then add the honey and cinnamon. Stir until bubbling.

❷ Add the bananas and cook for 1 minute, stirring to coat in the honey mixture. Pour in the orange juice and cook for 1 minute longer to make a sauce.

❸ Divide between four bowls and serve immediately with a scoop of ice cream per person.

White chocolate creams with cranberries

Takes 10 minutes + 2–3 hours chilling

12½ *POINTS* values per recipe

178 calories per serving

Serves 4

The cranberry compote looks like heaps of little jewels on top of the white chocolate creams. If you can't find cranberries, this dessert tastes just as good made with 100 g (3½ oz) frozen blueberries, for the same *POINTS* values.

450 ml (16 fl oz) skimmed milk
1 x 12 g sachet gelatine
100 g (3½ oz) frozen cranberries
40 g (1½ oz) caster sugar
50 g (1¾ oz) white chocolate, grated
150 g (5½ oz) low fat natural yogurt

❶ In a small bowl, pour in 4 tablespoons of the skimmed milk, sprinkle over the gelatine and leave to soak for 5 minutes.

❷ Place the cranberries in a small lidded saucepan with 15 g (½ oz) caster sugar and 1 tablespoon of water. Cover and cook for 4–5 minutes until they start to pop. Set aside to cool.

❸ In a separate saucepan, heat the rest of the milk until almost simmering. Remove from the heat and stir in the soaked gelatine, white chocolate and remaining sugar until dissolved. Cool quickly by standing the pan in cold water.

❹ In a mixing bowl, pour in the yogurt and gradually stir in the white chocolate milk. Pour into four dessert glasses, cover and chill in the fridge for 2–3 hours until set firm.

❺ Serve topped with the cranberry compote.

Blueberry crumbles

(Y) Takes 5 minutes to prepare, 20 minutes to cook
15 *POINTS* values per recipe
221 calories per serving
Serves 4

350 g (12 oz) frozen blueberries
1 tablespoon cornflour
60 g (2 oz) soft light brown sugar
75 g (2¾ oz) plain flour
40 g (1½ oz) low fat polyunsaturated margarine
25 g (1 oz) porridge oats

❶ In a bowl, toss the blueberries together with the cornflour and 25 g (1 oz) of the sugar. Divide between four small ovenproof dishes or ramekins and add 1 tablespoon of water to each dish.
❷ In a separate bowl, sift the flour and rub in the margarine until the mixture looks like breadcrumbs. Stir in the remaining sugar and the oats, then press the crumble mixture on top of the blueberries.
❸ Place the dishes on a baking tray and bake in the oven for 20 minutes until the crumble is golden and crisp, and the blueberry juices are bubbling up from underneath.

Apple bread pudding

(Y) Takes 5 minutes to prepare, 25 minutes to cook
9 *POINTS* values per recipe
181 calories per serving
Serves 4

This is best made with slightly stale bread so it's ideal for using up the end of a loaf in the bread bin. Instead of buying apple sauce, you can make it by chopping an apple, cooking it in a little water and then mashing it.

low fat cooking spray
200 g (7 oz) low fat vanilla flavour yogurt
1 egg, beaten
½ teaspoon ground mixed spice
100 g (3½ oz) apple sauce
25 g (1 oz) soft light brown sugar
100 g (3½ oz) crustless white or wholemeal bread, diced
1 apple, cored and diced

❶ Preheat the oven to Gas Mark 4/180°C/fan oven 160°C. Spray a baking dish with low fat cooking spray. Reserve half the yogurt to serve. In a bowl, mix the remaining yogurt together with the beaten egg, mixed spice, apple sauce and sugar.
❷ Stir the bread into the mixture, mixing well to coat, then stir in the apple. Spoon into the baking dish and bake in the oven for 25 minutes until firm, with a golden brown crispy top.
❸ Serve with the reserved vanilla yogurt drizzled over the hot pudding.

A truly comforting pudding.

scrumptious

Planning your week ahead: Chapter six

Dairy

- Cheddar cheese, half fat, 60 g
- Eggs, 3
- Fromage frais, low fat, 4 tbsp
- Low fat soft cheese, 150 g
- Mozzarella cheese, soft, reduced fat, 75 g
- Milk, skimmed, 515 ml
- Yogurt, Greek, 0% fat, 300 g
- Yogurt, low fat, natural, 150 g

Dry and canned ingredients

- Artichoke hearts in water, 1 x 400 g can
- Black bean sauce, 1 x 195 g jar
- Bread, white or wholemeal (for 60 g breadcrumbs)
- Caster sugar, 25 g

- Ciabatta, 1 loaf (300 g)
- Egg noodles, dried medium, 125 g
- Jelly, sugar free orange, 1 x 12 g sachet
- Penne, dried, 250 g
- Pesto sauce, 5 tbsp
- Redcurrant jelly, 2 tbsp
- Rosemary, dried, ½ tsp
- Soft flour tortillas, medium, 3
- Tomatoes, chopped, 1 x 400 g can

Fruit, vegetables and herbs

- Bananas, small, 2
- Blueberries, fresh, 75 g
- Broccoli, 175 g
- Butternut squash, 450 g
- Carrots, 4
- Cauliflower, 1
- Cherry tomatoes, 250 g

- Courgettes, 2
- Orange, 1
- Parsnips, 880 g
- Peppers, 2 red, 1 yellow, 1 green
- Raspberries, fresh, 100 g
- Red onion, 1
- Salad, crispy leaf, 150 g
- Spinach, young leaf, 200 g
- Spring onions, 3 bunches
- Strawberries, fresh, 500 g
- Sugar snap peas, 200 g
- Thyme, fresh, 1 x 25 g packet
- Tomatoes, 3
- Wild rocket leaves, 40 g

Meat and vegetarian alternatives

- Bacon, lean back, 4 rashers
- Chicken breasts, cooked, skinless and boneless, 2 x 150 g
- Chicken breasts, uncooked, skinless and boneless, 2 x 150 g
- Lamb leg steaks, lean, 4 x 100 g
- Pork sausages, low fat, thick, 8
- Quorn Chicken Style Pieces, 1 x 350 g packet

And from your Kitchen Basics, you will need the following ingredients: balsamic vinegar, black peppercorns, cocoa powder, dried mixed herbs, extra light mayonnaise, garlic, gravy granules, ground cinnamon, low fat cooking spray, onions, plain flour, reduced sugar strawberry jam and salt.

Pesto chicken salad

Takes 10 minutes

11½ *POINTS* values per recipe

246 calories per serving

Serves 4

200 g (7 oz) sugar snap peas, halved across

2 tablespoons pesto sauce

150 g (5½ oz) 0% fat Greek yogurt

2 tablespoons extra light mayonnaise e.g. Weight
    Watchers or Hellmann's

2 x 150 g (5½ oz) cooked skinless boneless chicken
    breasts, diced

1 red pepper, de-seeded and cut into short strips

150 g (5½ oz) crispy leaf salad

salt and freshly ground black pepper

❶ Bring a saucepan of water to the boil and cook the
sugar snap peas for 2 minutes until tender but still with
some bite, then drain and rinse in cold water.

❷ In a bowl, mix the pesto sauce together with the
yogurt and mayonnaise, adding seasoning to taste.

❸ Stir in the diced chicken, pepper and sugar snap
peas. Serve on a bed of crispy leaf salad.

Spinach and bacon salad with garlic croûtons

Takes 20 minutes

9 *POINTS* values per recipe

180 calories per serving

Serves 4

75 g (2¾ oz) ciabatta, diced

1 garlic clove, crushed

low fat cooking spray

4 rashers lean back bacon, chopped

2 bunches spring onions, chopped roughly

250 g (9 oz) cherry tomatoes, halved

2 tablespoons balsamic vinegar

200 g (7 oz) young leaf spinach

salt and freshly ground black pepper

❶ Preheat the oven to Gas Mark 6/200°C/fan oven
180°C. Toss the diced ciabatta with the garlic. Season
and spray with low fat cooking spray. Spread out on a
baking tray and bake in the oven for 8 minutes until crisp
and golden.

❷ While the croûtons are cooking, heat a non stick
frying pan. Spray with low fat cooking spray, add the
bacon and fry for 3 minutes until golden brown.

❸ Add the spring onions to the pan and fry for 1 minute,
then stir in the tomatoes and balsamic vinegar. Season
with freshly ground black pepper and stir fry for 2
minutes.

❹ Divide the spinach between four plates or bowls, then
spoon the hot bacon mixture over the leaves. Scatter the
crisp croûtons on to the salads and serve immediately.

Ⓨ **Tip** For a vegetarian version, replace the bacon with
75 g (2¾ oz) Quorn Deli Bacon Style Rashers, for a
POINTS value of 1 per serving.

Serve this warm salad as soon as it's ready to enjoy all the satisfying flavours at their best.

Pizza style bruschetta

Ⓨ Takes 15 minutes
14 *POINTS* values per recipe
217 calories per serving
Serves 4

Serve with a mixed zero *POINTS* value leaf salad, tossed with fat free vinaigrette dressing. Use a 300 g (10½ oz) ciabatta but you can reserve 75 g to make the croûtons in the Spinach and bacon salad on page 82.

225 g (8 oz) ciabatta (see introduction)
1 garlic clove, halved
3 ripe tomatoes, chopped roughly
1 x 400 g can artichoke hearts in water, drained and
quartered
75 g (2¾ oz) reduced fat soft mozzarella, diced
1 tablespoon fresh thyme leaves
salt and freshly ground black pepper

❶ Preheat the grill to a medium setting. Slice the ciabatta in half horizontally, then cut each section into two pieces. Toast lightly on both sides under the grill, then rub the garlic on to the cut sides of the toasted bread.

❷ In a bowl, mix the chopped tomatoes with seasoning then press these on to the ciabatta. Top with the pieces of artichoke heart, mozzarella and thyme. Season lightly with freshly ground black pepper, then grill for 4–5 minutes until the cheese is bubbling and golden.

Cheesy chicken penne with rocket

Takes 20 minutes

23½ *POINTS* values per recipe

413 calories per serving

Serves 4

Serve with a tomato salad, for no additional *POINTS* values.

250 g (9 oz) dried penne

175 g (6 oz) broccoli, broken into small florets

low fat cooking spray

2 x 150 g (5½ oz) skinless boneless chicken breasts, cut into small pieces

3 tablespoons pesto sauce

75 g (2¾ oz) low fat soft cheese

40 g (1½ oz) wild rocket leaves

❶ Bring a saucepan of water to the boil and cook the pasta for 10–12 minutes or according to the packet instructions until tender, adding the broccoli for the last 3 minutes of the cooking time.

❷ Heat a non stick frying pan and spray with low fat cooking spray. Stir fry the chicken for about 8 minutes over a medium heat until golden brown and cooked through.

❸ Drain the pasta and broccoli, reserving a little of the cooking water. Return to the pan and mix in the pesto, soft cheese and 4 tablespoons of the cooking water until evenly coated.

❹ Stir in the chicken and the rocket leaves, then serve immediately in warmed bowls.

Ⓨ Tip For a vegetarian version, replace the chicken with 300 g (10½ oz) Quorn Chicken Style Pieces, for the same *POINTS* values. The Quorn Chicken Style Pieces will only need to cook for 4–5 minutes in step 2.

Cauliflower provençale

Y Takes 20 minutes to prepare, 10 minutes to cook

5½ *POINTS* values per recipe

157 calories per serving

Serves 4

Serve with a medium jacket potato (225 g/8 oz) per person, for an additional *POINTS* value of 2½ per person.

low fat cooking spray

2 courgettes, quartered lengthways

3 garlic cloves, crushed

1½ teaspoons dried mixed herbs

1 x 400 g can chopped tomatoes

100 ml (3½ fl oz) boiling water

1 cauliflower, broken into large florets

60 g (2 oz) fresh breadcrumbs

60 g (2 oz) half fat Cheddar cheese, grated

salt and freshly ground black pepper

❶ Preheat the oven to Gas Mark 7/220°C/fan oven 200°C.

❷ Heat a lidded saucepan and spray with low fat cooking spray. Slice the courgette quarters into chunky pieces and fry for 3 minutes until coloured, then add 2 garlic cloves and 1 teaspoon of the mixed herbs. Cook for a further minute.

❸ Stir in the tomatoes with the courgettes and pour in the boiling water. Season, then mix in the cauliflower. Cover the pan and simmer for 10 minutes until the cauliflower is tender.

❹ In a bowl, mix the breadcrumbs and cheese together with the remaining garlic and mixed herbs.

❺ Transfer the cauliflower and sauce to an ovenproof dish and scatter the breadcrumb mixture all over. Mist with low fat cooking spray, then bake for 10 minutes until crisp and golden. Serve immediately.

Noodle pancakes with black bean Quorn

Y Takes 20 minutes

18½ *POINTS* values per recipe

333 calories per serving

Serves 4

125 g (4½ oz) dried medium egg noodles

50 g (1¾ oz) plain flour

1 egg

2 tablespoons skimmed milk

1 bunch spring onions, chopped roughly

low fat cooking spray

1 x 350 g packet Quorn Chicken Style Pieces

3 mixed peppers, de-seeded and chopped roughly

1 x 195 g jar black bean sauce

salt and freshly ground black pepper

❶ Bring a saucepan of water to the boil and cook the noodles for 4 minutes. Meanwhile, in a bowl, whisk the flour, egg and milk together with seasoning to make a thick batter. Drain the noodles, rinse in cold water, then snip into short lengths using scissors and stir into the batter with half the spring onions.

❷ Heat a non stick frying pan and spray with low fat cooking spray. Spoon half the noodle mixture into the pan as four separate pancakes and fry for 2½ minutes on each side over a high heat. Keep warm while you use the remaining mixture to make another four pancakes.

❸ Meanwhile, spray a separate non stick frying pan or wok with low fat cooking spray. Stir fry the Quorn and peppers for 5 minutes. Add the remaining spring onions to the pan, followed by the black bean sauce and 150 ml (5 fl oz) water. Simmer for 5 minutes, then serve two pancakes each with the Quorn mixture spooned over.

Savoury black bean sauce is delicious with crunchy mixed peppers. Noodle and spring onion pancakes complete the meal.

Sausages with roasted vegetable Yorkshires

Takes 50 minutes
18½ *POINTS* values per recipe
397 calories per serving
Serves 4

A real treat for a chilly night, this hearty recipe is particularly good served with a heap of lightly steamed green cabbage, for no additional *POINTS* values.

4 carrots, peeled and chopped into 2 cm (¾ inch) chunks
4 parsnips (180 g/6 oz), peeled and chopped into
    2 cm (¾ inch) chunks
450 g (1 lb) butternut squash, peeled, de-seeded, and
    chopped into 2 cm (¾ inch) chunks
low fat cooking spray
60 g (2 oz) plain flour
1 egg
150 ml (5 fl oz) skimmed milk
1 onion, chopped roughly
8 thick low fat pork sausages such as Weight Watchers
    Premium Pork Sausages
4 teaspoons gravy granules
250 ml (9 fl oz) boiling water
salt and freshly ground black pepper

❶ Preheat the oven to Gas Mark 7/220°C/fan oven 200°C. Spread the vegetables out on a large baking tray, season with freshly ground black pepper and spray lightly with low fat cooking spray. Roast in the oven for 15 minutes on the middle shelf.

❷ To make the Yorkshire pudding batter, sift the flour into a mixing bowl and make a well in the centre. Add the egg, then gradually mix in the milk to give a smooth batter. Season and set aside.

❸ When the 15 minutes are up, stir the onion in with the other vegetables and add the sausages to the tray. Return to the oven and cook for 5 minutes. At the same time, pop an 8 inch square tin or a four hole Yorkshire pudding tin on the top shelf to preheat.

❹ When the tin is hot, quickly spray with low fat cooking spray then pour in the batter and return to the oven. Cook above the tray of sausages and vegetables for 15 minutes until risen and crisp and the sausages are cooked.

❺ Meanwhile, make up the gravy granules with boiling water, following the packet instructions.

❻ Divide the Yorkshire pudding into four, (or serve one Yorkshire pudding each) and pile the roasted vegetables on to the Yorkshire puddings. Serve each one with two sausages, with the gravy poured over.

Ⓨ Tip For a vegetarian alternative, replace the pork sausages with Quorn sausages, and use vegetarian gravy granules, for a *POINTS* value of 4 per serving.

Balsamic glazed lamb with parsnip purée

Takes 20 minutes
18½ *POINTS* values per recipe
302 calories per serving
Serves 4

Serve with rocket, for no additional ***POINTS*** values.

700 g (1 lb 9 oz) parsnips, peeled, cores removed and
    chopped roughly
4 x 100 g (3½ oz) lean lamb leg steaks
low fat cooking spray
1 red onion, sliced
½ teaspoon dried rosemary
2 tablespoons balsamic vinegar
2 tablespoons redcurrant jelly
4 tablespoons skimmed milk
salt and freshly ground black pepper

❶ Bring a saucepan of water to the boil and cook the parsnips for 10 minutes or until soft.

❷ Meanwhile, heat a non stick frying pan and season the lamb. Spray the frying pan with low fat cooking spray and add the lamb. Scatter the red onion around the lamb and sprinkle in the rosemary. Cook for 3 minutes on each side over a high heat, stirring the onions around when you turn the lamb.

❸ Add the balsamic vinegar, redcurrant jelly and 2 tablespoons of water to the frying pan. Bubble for 2 minutes, turning the lamb to glaze it in the sauce.

❹ Drain the parsnips and mash with the milk. Serve the parsnip purée with the lamb steaks and spoon the red onions and sauce over the top.

Cinnamon tortilla chips with berry salsa

2½ POINTS VALUE

Takes 15 minutes
10½ POINTS values per recipe
168 calories per serving
Serves 4

This unusual sweet version of tortilla chips and salsa is a great dessert to share.

25 g (1 oz) caster sugar
1 teaspoon ground cinnamon
3 medium soft flour tortillas
low fat cooking spray
100 g (3½ oz) raspberries
200 g (7 oz) strawberries, trimmed and diced
75 g (2¾ oz) blueberries
150 g (5½ oz) 0% fat Greek yogurt

❶ Preheat the oven to Gas Mark 4/180°C/fan oven 160°C.

❷ In a bowl, mix together the sugar and cinnamon and then measure out 2 teaspoons (for the salsa) and transfer to another bowl.

❸ Spray both sides of each tortilla with low fat cooking spray, and sprinkle with the cinnamon sugar. Using kitchen scissors, cut each tortilla into four strips, then snip the strips into small triangles. Spread out on a large baking tray and bake for 6–7 minutes until crisp.

❹ To make the berry salsa, put the raspberries into a bowl with the reserved cinnamon sugar and lightly crush using a fork. Stir in the strawberries and the whole blueberries. Serve with the cinnamon tortilla chips for dipping, and the yogurt on the side.

Chocolate orange pots

Takes 10 minutes + 2 hours chilling

5 *POINTS* values per recipe

71 calories per serving

Serves 4

A classic flavour combination, these chocolate orange pots taste similar to the filling in a delicious cheesecake, but have far fewer *POINTS* values per serving.

200 ml (7 fl oz) boiling water

1 x 12 g sachet sugar free orange jelly

15 g (½ oz) cocoa

150 ml (5 fl oz) skimmed milk

75 g (2¾ oz) low fat soft cheese

150 g (5½ oz) low fat natural yogurt

❶ Put the boiling water into a measuring jug and sprinkle over the jelly crystals. Make up to 300 ml (10 fl oz) with cold water.

❷ In a bowl, tip in the cocoa and gradually stir in the milk, until you have a smooth paste.

❸ In a separate mixing bowl, whisk the soft cheese and yogurt together, then mix in the cocoa milk, followed by the orange jelly. Pour into four ramekins or small bowls.

❹ Cover and chill for 2 hours or until firmly set.

Strawberry and banana crêpes

Ⓨ Takes 15 minutes

12½ *POINTS* values per recipe

194 calories per serving

Serves 4

50 g (1¾ oz) plain flour

a pinch of salt

1 egg, beaten

125 ml (4 fl oz) skimmed milk

grated zest and juice of ½ an orange

low fat cooking spray

75 g (2¾ oz) reduced sugar strawberry jam

300 g (10½ oz) strawberries, trimmed and quartered

2 small bananas, sliced

4 tablespoons low fat fromage frais, to serve

❶ In a mixing bowl, sift the flour and salt. Whisk in the egg, followed by the milk, to give a smooth batter. Stir in the orange zest.

❷ Preheat a non stick frying pan. Spray with low fat cooking spray then swirl in one quarter of the pancake batter to coat the base of the pan. Cook for 1–2 minutes, turning halfway, until golden. Remove to a plate and keep warm while you repeat with the remaining batter to make three more pancakes, spraying the pan each time you make a pancake.

❸ Meanwhile, in a separate non stick saucepan, gently heat the jam with 2 tablespoons of the orange juice to make a sauce.

❹ In a bowl, mix the strawberries and sliced bananas together with the remaining orange juice.

❺ To serve, fill each pancake with a quarter of the fruit mixture, then fold in half. Drizzle the strawberry sauce over the pancakes and top with a spoonful of fromage frais.

Pancakes are always a popular pudding – no need to save them for Shrove Tuesday.

Index by POINTS values